Uber
GOD

Driving Out of the Darkness

KARL GERTZ

ISBN 978-1-0980-2466-6 (paperback)
ISBN 978-1-0980-2467-3 (digital)

Christian Faith Publishing, Inc.
832 Park Avenue
Meadville, PA 16335
www.christianfaithpublishing.com

Printed in the United States of America

Foreword

L ove is a powerful phenomenon that changes lives. In fact, we were designed in love and for love. When God blew His breath of life into the lungs of man, His breath of perfect love established an intimate bond between the Creator and His creation for the first time. Man was created in true intimacy. All of heaven rejoiced over God's magnificent creation of man and the intricate details that were formed in love. His creation prospered and was one with Him. Then man rebelled against this intimacy and all creation was silenced, separating man from His perfect love. Since that time, mankind has been searching for security in love. For many, we have put our hope in the world and all of the temporary solutions established to fulfill our need for love. We have twisted true intimacy with physical pleasure and have lost the essence and the heart of God in intimacy. True intimacy is found in perfect love, and this love is fulfilled by the presence of God and God alone.

First Corinthians 13:13 states, "And now abide faith, hope and love, these three; but the greatest of these is love." Intimacy is a place of exchange. As we draw near to the Father, He draws near to us. All that is ours becomes His, and all that is His becomes ours. We become one in our interaction with the Holy Spirit in the secret place of intimacy. However, this place of exchange is one of love, not duty. Our sense of duty found in faith is the fruit of love, not the motivator of love. If intimacy is nothing more than duty or religion, then we will become bored and tired, and move away from trust and intimacy with God. However, if our intimacy is full of passion for God's presence, then it will be vibrant, full of life, and we will long for more of Him.

Love must be the motivator from which we enter into an intimate encounter with the whole Godhead. Love is the foundation from which we live and demonstrate the Kingdom. I have ministered to many people who do not understand love or how to be loved, and any discussion of love is lost in confusion and self-condemnation. In doing so, they spend more time trying to control love and keep from being loved than really experiencing the fullness and freedom in love. In this cycle of hurt, they find themselves alone, tired, and weighed down by the heaviness of pain, always yearning for something (someone) to love and accept them.

Romans 5:5 states, "Now hope does not disappoint, because the love of God has been poured out in our hearts by the Holy Spirit who was given to us." Love gives birth to hope and hope produces our faith. God so loved the world He gave His only begotten Son! God is love! God is the Perfect Love that drives out fear. Love bears all things, believes all things, hopes all things, endures all things; love never fails! God will capture your heart; He will meet you in the intimacy of His presence and overwhelm you with His unconditional, never-failing eternal love! The greatest testimony of all that Jesus accomplished in His earthly ministry is that He loved! Testimony after testimony records Jesus touching the untouchable, dining with the sinners, healing the destitute, loving the poor, and bringing hope to the hopeless. Jesus said, "He who has seen Me has seen the Father" (John 14:9). Jesus was the full expression of the Father's love for mankind to experience. The will of God is for all His creation to experience the depth, width, length, and height of His amazing, unfailing, unending love. Intimacy becomes the place of exchange between Perfect Love and His most prized possession—you.

When we are captured by the love of God, our hunger and passion cannot be quenched. We find ourselves, like children in His midst, full of innocence, trust, and expectation for something new and more. This unmovable, unshakeable, undeniable love compels us to serve, obey, and love even more. This is the New Covenant truth realized. We have been restored to an epic love affair between the Creator and His most valuable creation. Jesus is our perfect example of this love and intimacy! Jesus was the fulfillment of what Adam lost! Jesus not only restored us to right relationship with God, but He showed how to live this life in perfect intimacy with Him! This is the great invitation. "Come and love Me, choose Me that I may release in you My fullness, " says the Lord!

Uber God is an amazing testimony of the love of God and His influence over many people's lives. Karl shares his story in such a way that it draws you into the truth of God's redeeming love. This book will move you to tears and make you laugh as you journey with Karl through the process of becoming a child of God and encountering true love. Karl reveals the secrets of the great exchange of love and security. When we are captured by the love of God, we become His instrument of truth, and Karl wonderfully illustrates this truth in his testimonies of being an Uber driver who allows God to invade his car and touch lives. Karl has said yes to the great invitation and has allowed the fullness of God to be experienced in his world. *Uber God* is a powerful truth of intentionally making love a lifestyle.

Pastor David Carlson
Josiah Center
St. Paul, Minnesota

Acknowledgments

I am so thankful to so many people who carried me, fed me, housed me, and just plain old loved me, and at times believed in me and my God-given ability to bring forth my story in a way that is honorable to the people in my book and to our heavenly Father.

Thank you to my sister Cheryl and her husband, Ric, for giving me a place to stay and rest my heavy heart. Also to Anthony (Du Renza) for always showering me with kindness and love and shelter; you are truly light in the darkness. To all my friends at Josiah Center: Linda, Barb, Michael, Susan, and Mary, and the leadership of both Doug Stanton and Dave Carlson and their amazing wives. God put you in my life so I could see Him thank you for showing me love during the darkest time in my life. To Brian, Kevin, Tim, and their beautiful spouses, your support every day through your time, your heart, and patience will never be forgotten. I love you guys.

Thank you to all my brothers and sisters and so many friends who have been there for me as I maneuvered through turbulent times. I would have a hard time naming them all, but where I owe the most honor and praise and thanks is to Jesus, my one and only who I know will never leave me or forsake me. All thanks to You, my UBER GOD!

Introduction

I am a simple guy with simple thoughts, but I have a true love for God and genuine, heartfelt feelings for other people; most of all for my family. As we take this adventure, my point is and will always be that, regardless of the situation, our God, our Father, is always there.

I will show you as I walk through the toughest part of my life that my Lord and Savior Jesus was always there. I will also show how God has been there for others through me, as I drove them from point A to point B, and all points in between. My God has no boundaries. His love for His kids is overwhelming. He has picked me up when I have been at my very lowest and provided for me when I didn't have the strength to take care of myself. He doesn't have to, but He proves Himself over and over, how much He loves me and loves all of His children. The same way He tells us not to hide our light but to stand up on the hill so everyone can see it. I have tried to do that in my life and from my car.

So, jump into the backseat of my 2016 Kia Soul, put on your seatbelt, open your ears, grab a tissue, and prepare your heart for what God has done for me, through my whole life, while I drive down Glory Road serving my Uber God!

My Perfect Kiss

On a cold December night twenty years ago, a soft, light snowfall slowly cascaded to the ground through the twinkling lights of downtown Minneapolis. We were headed to a restaurant called Basils, a fancy little place off Eighth and the Nicollet Mall in the IDS Center. We had parked a couple of blocks away and were walking down the mall. It was cold, and we had just stopped at a light and were waiting to cross the street. I looked at you, gorgeous from head to toe in a little black dress, shoes with a heel but nothing too crazy, your coat and every bit of you just lightly covered in snow, my perfect angel. The moment took me away, I couldn't resist the opportunity to kiss the most beautiful woman I'd ever seen. In the moments it took me to get close to you my heart started pounding. I felt this would be something special, something that I might never experience ever again.

It started fast; I turned toward you, the lights from the holiday decorations and the fifty-plus stories of office buildings towered over us as it all softly reflected off your beautiful eyes. I moved close to you, wearing just a sports coat and slacks, not dressed properly for the weather. I reached my arms around your waist and pulled you close; you looked up at me…a snowflake landed on your cheek. I could feel the warmth of your breath before our lips ever touched, and when they did touch, I never wanted them to leave. It seemed as if time stopped. I'm sure it didn't last more than a few seconds, but that short period of time sticks out in my mind like it lasted for an hour.

The rest of our night was great; we were celebrating your twenty-first birthday. Sadly I don't remember the gift I got you, but I do know what I got that night. I got a kiss from the woman of my dreams that was so incredible that just the thought of that night and that kiss brings joy to my world. There's never been anyone else like you.

Beginning of July 2017

We are on the second day of a seven-day trip, at the Garden of the Gods, in Colorado Springs. It's already been a tough trip. I went on this trip hoping that my wife and I would be able to rekindle our struggling marriage. It's a hot day, eighty-plus degrees. Dawn and I had ridden out to the park with her parents in their new Jeep. I probably should've stayed at the house, because this day would involve a lot of walking, something I wasn't doing very well anymore. They got out of the car around ten in the morning. It was already very hot. I knew I didn't have much of a choice at this point but to go with them, but I had brought a book and was prepared to read. The interior of the car was dark, mostly black, I believe. It was boiling in the dry-dusty park that was dedicated to the gods. But all I could think about was: "When is the one true God going to step in and save the day for me, for Dawn, and our family?" I spent more time pleading with the God of the universe, to step in to take our lives, and point us in the right direction, more than anything else. I needed my Uber God.

I Am the Second

I am the second of twins. I had a twin sister, Kathryn Elaine Gertz. When I think of my childhood, I can't help but think of her. She was my best friend, as well as my sister; a constant companion. Growing up, she was always bigger, faster, and stronger than me…not a good combination for a brother. In many ways I was truly a little brother. I was always competing, either with my twin sister or my older brothers, and that was for everything, from sports, girls, money, to basic popularity. I was always trying to be a little bit better. Looking back, I may have thought I achieved that, but I certainly did not. I was so wrapped up in trying to please myself that I didn't really think about anyone else. But if I did think of anyone else, it was probably Kathy, and she did the same for me.

We were five years old. I remember the story like it was yesterday. Kathy and I had left our home and had gone to the park. It was a different day and age, and this wasn't so dangerous, or at least not as dangerous at the park as it was at home. Events that happened that day were scary and maybe just slightly funny. The park was about two blocks from our home. It's funny how well a mad voice can carry, even outside. We heard the scream of our mother, "Kathy, Karl," over and over. Kathy looked at me; a look of fright covered her face.

I'm sure it was on my face as well. We started to run home. I'm sure this is the one time Kathy would have preferred to not be the faster one. As we both ran all the way toward our house, she maneuvered her way around a gentleman who was walking down the sidewalk, in sandals, with a walking stick. He was a blur, that was gone in a flash. Kathy waited for me. As we both entered the house together, our mother had that look on her face. It would've scared most grown men, and on this day like so many other days, it terrified us.

As our mother walked around the kitchen area holding a spatula, slapping the counter, and screaming, we were both scared. We didn't know what Mom would do next. She had often resorted to whatever was handy to use as her next disciplinary device. Sometimes a spoon, belt, or a cord, but today she wielded a spatula. She screamed at both of us to get into the dining room. As we walked into the room, we could see that all but two chairs had been pushed away from the table.

Uber Guy, Super God, God of Miracles

It's October 1st-ish and it's the first Timberwolves game of the year. I pick up two guys in Apple Valley and start driving toward Minneapolis. These guys are excited about the upcoming basketball season, and maybe, just maybe, that the Timberwolves could break their thirteen-year drought of reaching the playoffs.

One gentleman said, "I see you only drive for Uber," and asked why I don't drive for Lyft as well. I smiled and said the name of the book is *Uber God*.

The other guy said, "You seem to be a good driver, but probably not the very best," while laughing and poking his buddy. I laughed as well, but I had to explain what I meant by the title of the book I was writing. I told him that, the same way I only drive for one company, I only serve the one true God. I told him about sharing the love of Jesus with everyone who got in my car and praying with a lot of them.

The first guy said, "How is that even possible, with all the political correctness? Don't you have to worry that you might offend someone?" I told him my example on how to treat others, always did it in a unoffensive way. He loved lepers, loved prostitutes, and tax collectors. He showed them all respect and unconditional love, and treated everyone with value. Jesus is my example, my super example, my super God, my Uber God! These guys loved the idea and loved the name of the book. I have only driven for Uber, the same way I will only serve one God. I won over some admiration and possibly a part of their hearts, which is good, considering the Timberwolves lost the game. God: one; world: zero. Game on. And so, began the telling of His story, for His glory! The story of my Uber God.

You shall have no other gods before Me.

—Exodus 20:2

Bond in Trauma

With our mom's face beet red, she screamed for us to sit in each of the chairs. My sister was the first to be tied up. She cried as my mother wrapped her arms, behind her back, with a vacuum cleaner cord. Just looking at my sister's face, I could feel the sting of tears on her cheeks, as she cried with confusion. She was scared because of what was happening; I was scared because I was next. After Kathy was firmly tied up, my mother left the room. I was hoping and praying that she would not come back. Sometimes being Mom's favorite had its rewards, but not today. Moments later, she came smashing through the door, with a long jump rope in her hand. She tied both my hands behind my back and then to the bottom of the chair. She was screaming to both of us, but directly in my face, "My name is Gertz, that's why it hurts!" over and over, almost like she was possessed. She screamed directly in my face, that neither one of us should make a single noise or we were going to get it. I felt like we were already getting it and we didn't know why. Anger comes with a sense of rage that oftentimes isn't coherent. We both sat there perfectly quiet, for more than an hour, barely looking at one another for fear that we might say something. After an hour, I looked up and saw my sister smiling at me. She slowly lifted her hand to show me she was free. I smiled back and lifted both of my hands.

Right at that moment we both saw a head of sandy blond hair rising at the window. It was my sister Sue. I'm not sure how she knew we were in the dining room, but my mother had locked the doors to the house and was sleeping on the couch, with the dog, strangely enough. The chaos that had been going on for a couple of hours died down. My sister banged on the door until Mom let her in. Sue instantly came into the dining room and in a makeshift kind of way freed us. This would be one of many times that Kathy and I were disciplined in a cruel and inhumane fashion. Incidents like this cemented our bond to love and watch out for one another. I was always there for her, and she was always there for me. We needed more; we need our Super God.

I'm still lost without you. I miss you, Kathy.

Dawn of an Old Day

I am now fifty years old. Between the ages of nineteen and twenty-six I had a relationship with another Dawn. Most of this relationship was not a committed relationship, and that was mostly my fault. I had told myself that I would never give my heart to another woman, ever again. We were both pretty heavy drinkers, we had a lot of good times together, but a lot of hard times as well. Through this whole relationship, I was never faithful, and sometimes neither was she. Five years into our difficult relationship, we became pregnant with my oldest daughter, Kalie.

I remember the day that Dawn went to labor. We were going to her uncle Dave's apartment. As we were heading toward the front door the sprinklers came on and blasted the both of us. I didn't know at the time that it also sent Kalie's mom into a pre-labor situation. We spent a couple hours at her uncle's apartment, and then I asked to go hang out with my friends. I went to the bar, she went home and eventually went into full labor, while I was getting drunk, fairly typical for me at that time. I did make it to the hospital with many hours to spare, but I should've been there earlier and I shouldn't have gotten there with a headache.

To that point, there had never been a more exciting time in my life. I thought perhaps on that day I would change, I would become a better person, a better man, a better dad than what I had—but that would not be the case. It didn't take long for my cheating ways and heavy drinking to return to my life, sometimes with a vengeance. At some point she grew tired of the type of person I was, both for herself and for our daughter.

After living together for more than two years, she said it was time for her to leave. I didn't take it well. I realized that the one consistent person in my life was saying goodbye. I quit eating, started drinking a lot. In September 1995, I was pulled over and received a DWI. I thought my life was tough, but now I just made it so much tougher. It would take a while for things to get better. Losing the best people in my life wasn't about to end soon. At this point, I didn't even realize, I was in need of my Uber God.

But because of His great love for us, God, who is rich in mercy, made us alive with Christ even when we were dead in transgressions—it is by grace you have been saved.

—Ephesians 2:4–5

Looking to the Sky

It's the 29th of September, the sun is bright, it's pretty warm, and it's just about the end of my day. I'm in St. Paul and my phone indicates that I have a run. The address tells me I will be picking up my rider, right off the Mississippi River. There are very nice houses in the area.

I pull up in front of the house and waited. After a couple minutes, as I call, the phone starts to ring. A young lady comes walking out the front door. She is walking quickly, staring at the ground. Just before she gets to my car, she looks up and gives me a courtesy smile. I could tell something wasn't quite right. She was beautiful, tall, maybe six feet, with dark, kinky, shoulder-length hair, with the complexion of possibly a mix of African-American, Hispanic with a touch of Scandinavian.

I start out with some small talk, which I'm pretty good at, and asked if she was from that area. She said she wasn't, she was visiting a friend. I asked her name, she said her name was Sky. "Cool name," I replied, and then she asked my name, and asked if I had kids. I said that I did and told her the breakdown: three girls and two boys, and their ages. She at that point told me she was on her way to go talk to her parents, about what, she never told me, but she was nervous and I could tell this wasn't an easy trip for her. I then told her that I was a Christian and that at different times my children have done things that were against the law, could've hurt themselves, someone else or me. I told her it never would matter what they had done, because with all my heart, I love them and would do anything for them. There is nothing that I would not forgive them for, they are my kids, the same way our heavenly Father would do anything for us and already has.

As I looked up into the mirror, I could see her dark brown eyes. They seemed a little sad, and I don't know if my words were any source of comfort. Our ride together got very quiet. I knew before she got out of the car today, I would ask her if I could pray for her situation. Oftentimes God steps in and knocks on the door of their hearts before we ever say a word, that's one way we know it's God. When we pulled up in front of her parents' house, she looked up and asked me if I would pray for her situation. I think she thought that prayer wouldn't happen right away, but that's not how I do things. We prayed. I asked the Lord for peace, joy, and wisdom to do and say the right thing. When she left my car, the smile on her face told me the joy of the Lord would be her strength. Praise to You, my Uber God!

Casting all your cares [all your anxieties, all your worries, and all your concerns, once and for all] on Him, for He cares about you [with deepest affection, and watches over you very carefully].

—1 Peter 5:7 (AMP)

You're Still the One

My sister Kathy and I still remain very close, although it seemed at times we didn't see each other as much. I always knew she was there for me, especially now with my break-up with Dawn #1. In some ways, I relied on my sister more and more. That wouldn't take long to change.

Kathy called me one day and asked if I would go with her to the doctor, she was worried. She had this bump on her leg that she felt was just a bruise from being bumped, pushing a cart that she used at work every day. On this day we went to the doctor, and he did not confirm his thoughts but he told us that he thought Kathy had bone cancer. His diagnosis was right on, right from the start. This would begin a long battle that Kathy would end up losing.

Over the next three years, there were lots of ups and downs, both with Kathy's health and my own situations. After my DWI, I had to take another job. I used to drive for a living, but that was no longer an option. I started working for a fastener company for about half of what I used to make. Now, I had twice the bills, so I was also working at a detail shop two nights a week, cleaning cars. Keeping busy helped me not think about what was going on in my life or Kathy's.

As much as I wanted to only think about myself, I had a twin sister who needed me. Her boyfriend of ten years, at this point, was more worried and consumed with music and partying than Kathy's condition, and in some ways, I tried to fill in where he didn't. Taking the kids to dance or hockey was one of those ways, other ways were selling candy bars for her son Derek's hockey team. It's crazy to think how chocolate can change your whole world.

You're still the one that makes me strong,
still the one I want to take along;
We're still having fun, 'cause you're still the one…

—Orleans, "Still the One"

Frustration

It was fairly hot and a little humid in my great big lonely bedroom in Colorado Springs. What a pain in the arse it had been, just getting into bed each night. The bed was a bit high for me, who couldn't jump or lift my one leg very much at all. The first night, I ended up sleeping kind of sideways with my legs hanging off the edge of the bed. Every night after that, I stepped onto my towel- and blanket-filled suitcase, to get my butt up high enough to position my broken body, which was in a better place than my heart…comfort is not always my final objective. I'm frustrated and tired and needed my powerful Savior. I need my Uber God!

I have said these things to you, that in Me you may have peace. In the world you will have tribulation. But take heart; I have overcome the world.

—John 16:33

Feeling the Shift

It's the last week in August 2007, I am having struggles with my health. Things are happening that I can't figure out. I've always been a very athletic person, but I found myself, in the last ten years or so, not being able to do things as well or at all, like I used to be able to. I thought perhaps I was just getting old. I've always been a strong runner and at some level enjoyed it, but in the last year or so while I ran, my right foot kept skipping on the ground. I thought that I just needed to stretch a little more and sometimes stretching did help, but recently, I could not run at all. My foot would dive straight down, toe first into the ground. I had recently split my toe open, while we were at the cabin playing volleyball. I started to run after the ball and smashed my toe directly down into the tar, on the driveway near the volleyball court. I remember saying something to Dawn, that perhaps I should go see a doctor, so I did.

I went to go see Dr. Wienke, a very nice guy and a doctor whom I trusted, because recently he had diagnosed my sister-in-law's cancer when the other doctors had repeatedly given her a wrong diagnosis. He was a no-nonsense kind of man, a stick-to-the-basics-and-figure-it-out guy. I was hoping that's what I needed as well. When I saw him, he really didn't have any answers for me and he suggested that I go see a neurologist. As much as he didn't have answers, I feel that maybe he knew.

From the moment the doctor walked into the room, I could almost tell she had an idea. Dr. Li (Lee), from the very first moments, told me that I favored my right side, that I barely use my right leg or right arm at all. She did some quick little reflex and little finger motion tapping test. She, at this point, said that in her estimation there was a pretty good chance that I had multiple sclerosis. Within a couple of short days, and after lots of tests, it was confirmed, and sadly in this day and age of the Internet, I received all sorts of gloom and doom stories and scenarios. I kept trying to find a positive side to my newly contracted life sentence, but you won't find it in stories about Richard Pryor or Terry Garr. In the end, I knew I had the love of my Creator, my children, and my wife, and, I guess I've heard, "two out of three ain't bad." My foundation was starting to shake.

Truly He is my rock and my salvation, He is my fortress, I WILL NOT BE SHAKEN.

—Psalm 62:6

Deer God

In my heart I've known for years I couldn't stand that another man was loving my wife, double betrayal. The obvious, my wife, whom I thought could at times walk on water. I elevated her a little higher than I should have, and the man who was a part of the deception was in our Bible study group. Someone I trusted, but in hindsight I should not have.

This goes beyond betrayal and into heart-breaking rejection, the kind that makes you think life is not worth living, the kind of frustration that makes driving off a bridge seem appealing as an end to the pain, but not an answer to the question of *Why?* Too many times, in too many ways, I've thought of ways to end my pain. The selfish word there is *my*; I wasn't thinking of others, not my kids, my siblings, or my friends. I guess by not following through, it shows that I was thinking of others or at the very least I was a coward.

I've always loved being out in the woods, mostly when it is legal to shoot and eat deer. The only bad part of that is, you kill deer with a gun, and having a gun in your hands while you're severely depressed is not a good combination. Thinking of my broken family in this broken world would start me thinking of the pain I would inflict on my kids and friends, and usually that was enough, but not always.

It the first week in November 2016, my friend Kevin and I were out hunting. Our hunting days always start early, up and at 'em by 4:30 a.m. Today it's just Kevin and me, and I'm struggling. The enemy is wreaking havoc in my head and on my heart. I'm missing the unity of a God-centered relationship with my wife. What I feel from her now is more that she despises me, that I'm holding her back, and I don't want to be that heavy anchor around her neck or the one person or thing that holds her back from anything. Me ending my life would free her from me and maybe end both our misery.

I know you don't make deals with God, but I'm at the end of my rope. I'm desperate and I need direction, so l start making my deal or plea with God.

It had been a slow hunting day, it's mid-afternoon, and neither Kevin nor I had seen a deer. I had been praying, asking, begging, pleading for restoration of my marriage, and then I started letting the enemy and his lies invade my mind. I know he only comes to steal, kill, and destroy. He had already stolen my wife, destroyed my family, and now he was trying his best to kill me.

I made my deal. I said, if I didn't see a deer during the rest of the day, I would end my misery, but if I did see a deer I would persevere, push on. This wasn't a deal with God or myself, it was a deal with the devil, and he honors these deals.

No sooner than I had finished my deal, I started rewriting it, flipping it around again and again. Confusion was getting the best of me, and confusion is not of God. In the end, I stuck with the original plan: if I did see a deer, I would push forward and try to continue to reconcile, but if I didn't see any deer, I was already formulating a plan to get Kevin to leave before me. I made the deal this way because I didn't believe we would see any deer that day.

For God is not the author of confusion but of peace...

—1 Corinthians 14:33 (NKJV)

Unseen Christmas

It's December 23rd, I'm picking up a man named Thomas, down in Bloomington. He called me just before I got to his house and gave me specific instructions on how to find him. I pulled up into his driveway and he started coming out with luggage. He opened the trunk and realized the suitcase would not fit in the back. He then opened the back door and set the luggage inside, looked up, and told me not to worry; his wife was sick, but not sick like a cold. She had just gone through a cancer treatment chemotherapy and was kind of feeling sick. I realized right then I would have another opportunity to pray with someone, but on this day, it would not be the person I thought it would be.

Thomas grabbed a couple more bags, and I saw a lady starting to head out the door. She walked very slowly. She was very well bundled up, had a coat that almost went to her feet, gloves and a scarf bundled around her. But even through all of this I could tell she was frail and weak. Thomas helped her in the car. He had a very soft and gentle voice. I could tell he was very patient in this terrible situation. It hadn't dimmed his undying love for his wife, Olga, and he showed incredible stamina, facing this never-ending battle against the dismantling of the body and the breaking of the heart. We had small talk in the car ride, and she told me they were going to see her son in Chicago. I could tell by her brief conversation about her son that she was very proud but also somewhat apprehensive. I'm sure her sickness gave her a sense of being a burden. I experience that every day, but God values us enough to die for us, and He did.

A few minutes had passed when I said to Olga, "You and I have something in common. We both walk with a cane." But then I said with a big smile that God has a perfect plan for our healing and that He knows everything that we need and want, before we ever ask. "He loves his children, He is a good father." She seemed very open to what I was saying and was becoming emotional. While this was going on, I saw Thomas fumbling through his pockets looking for something. I looked at him as we pulled up to the airport and he said he did not have his license and would have to go back home to get it. We realized that getting Olga into the airport would probably be the best plan. Thomas helped her get into a seat in the airport with their baggage and he came running back out. He got into my car and we took off. We had just taken a left out of the drop-off area when Thomas said, "I have some identification that I use for work in my suitcase." He was sure of it and that I should just bring him back.

The Minneapolis/St. Paul airport has a big loop and we were about to use it. I realized at that time, with everything that happened, I didn't get the opportunity to pray with Olga. I asked Thomas if I could pray for him and his wife. He said that he didn't believe in prayer, but if I wanted to, that would be OK. I started to pray for healing on his wife and prayed for Thomas to come to know the Lord as his personal Savior and that their relationship would become real. We finish the loop and Thomas jumped out of my car, ran through the doors to be who he always has been to the woman he loved. But hopefully, with the newfound relationship with our Creator. I drove away thinking that this whole ride was orchestrated by God, for Him. It's funny, the Bible talks about one Thomas, the doubter, who has become infamous for that one thing, doubt. I hope today is the beginning for this Thomas to never doubt the power of God and the love of God ever again.

I thought this ride would be all about the woman whom I could see was sick, but I think it ended up being about the man and about his needs. From where I sit in my Uber seat, I couldn't see what God's intentions for this trip were going to be, but from what I could see now, I know God is always good!

While we look not at the things which are seen, but we look at the things which are not seen; for the things which are seen are temporal, but the things which are not seen are eternal.

—2 Corinthians 4:18

A Whole New Dawn

Part of keeping costs down for hockey was selling candy bars. I felt like I was selling them everywhere I went. On this day in February, I had brought a case to work and I'd been selling them to everyone. I went into the front office to sell some more, and that's when I met a beautiful young lady who worked for another company in the same office. She was a young, smart, beautiful Christian, and single.

I did my very best to get her to buy a candy bar, but she didn't. I couldn't stop thinking about her. I went out of my way multiple times that day and in the days to come just to see her. When I heard from the other receptionist that she was asking questions about me, my heart jumped for joy. I don't think my heart has ever jumped for anyone else in my whole life. She was a big water drinker and would come out to the warehouse to get water a few times a day. Every time she did, she would get a heavy dose of stares from every man and boy in the warehouse. I fit somewhere in between there, man and boy, but from the very start, before I even knew if she knew I existed, she already had my heart. Little did she know that she was an answer from God to prayers I had been praying...

But seek first His kingdom and His righteousness,
and all these things will be given to you as well.

—Matthew 6:33

The End Is Deer

I rested in disbelief, not really understanding the deal I had just made, when I heard the snapping of a branch not far from me. I turned around as a great big doe came running directly toward my deer stand. I was excited as tears filled my eyes. I shot three times, and in typical Karl fashion, I missed, but My Uber God had spoken to me Loud and Clear, "Push on, My son; persevere. I have great plans for you."

It was a couple of minutes after my gunshots when I heard the footsteps of Kevin coming toward me. I was trying to compose myself, I didn't want him to see my tears. He walked up to my spot and started asking me what I had seen. When I started crying like a baby, he knew how lonely I had been and how much I loved Dawn. He set his gun against a tree and put his arms around me, and we hugged a long time; like brothers, or more than brothers, brothers who have fought together in Blaze Orange instead of camouflage. As I cried, I told him part of the story about my deal, that if I saw a deer, I would press on in my marriage, but I didn't tell him the part about killing myself. We didn't see any more deer that day, but it didn't matter, God had spoken to me. He said to persevere, to love someone even when they're not loving you. I think about how He feels, when He loves all of us so much, but we come across lying, cheating, and not being faithful to Him. I think in a small way I know how He feels. I'm sorry, God, please forgive me.

For weeks, months, and years, I have had different people praying for my situation, people who knew both Dawn and me, who didn't have a bias one way or the other, they just wanted us back together again. I think if we are praying into the will of God, it doesn't always turn out how we want it.

The same friends who were praying for my marriage were also petitioning to the Lord on my behalf for my life. They had slowly seen me deteriorate before their eyes.

I thank You, Jesus, for putting men of prayer into my life, and thank You for carrying their requests to the Father. I'll never doubt the power of prayer, or the power of Your Uber love!

You are my Uber God and You show Yourself through so many different circumstances and different ways in Your creation. Thank You for lifting me up and carrying me when I didn't have the strength!

...being strengthened with all power according to His glorious might, so that you may have great endurance and patience, giving joyful thanks to the Father...

—Colossians 1:11–12

The Walking Man

It's early June 1999, and we've been in our house almost two weeks. It's work all day and work way past sundown, it's getting old. We have been plastering walls and painting rooms and pulling off wallpaper, as well as tearing out carpet, for what seems like forever. I haven't even touched our yard. Besides the grass needing to be cut, the bushes that go across the front yard near the curb are begging for a trim. As I look out, I see the top of a red hat slowly bobbing up and down, probably three inches above the hedge, not moving fast but always steady. I see all of the guy as he passes the mailbox and turns slightly toward the walkway across the street.

He's a tall guy, wearing cutoff shorts, with black socks and sandals, and a faded T-shirt that at one time said something, but from here it just looked dirty. What sticks out to me the most is the walking stick he held in his right hand. It's huge: five, maybe six feet high. There are both light and dark swirls in the wood. As he moves across the circle, his speed never seems to change, very constant. As I stare at this long-legged, gangly man, I think at some point I'd like to meet him and hear his story, but now I've got a bathroom to prime. Back to work.

Finding My Way

Back to that answer-to-prayer thing I was talking about. During my mid-teens, I was involved with the Christian group called Timber Bay. At this time in my life, I had given my life to Christ. This was the first time I knew there was a Savior, a God who loved me, a God who would never leave me. And that "never leave me" part was huge, because even though He never left me, I left Him. I got caught up in the world and what was cool and what was cool to the rest of my world. I was a long-haired, Bon Jovi-looking, Mötley Crüe-loving, wannabe rocker. I could sing a little bit and I could look the part, but even if I wasn't a rocker, I could make all the girls think I was. And I did. I was a nice guy, fun, everybody liked me, as long as I wasn't your boyfriend. I was dishonest, cheated, hurt a lot of women, and pissed off a lot of guys. But there was a part of me that knew this was not what God intended for my life.

As my life spiraled downward, I started to pray. I prayed for a woman who knew the Lord, who was smart, fun, and beautiful. Dawn fit the bill perfectly. She was going through a rough point in her life as well. We both had young daughters, we were fairly new to our jobs, and she was recently divorced. I had never been so excited or so caught up in one person in my life. She was my gift from God. I didn't want to screw it up, but I am Karl, and I didn't know the right or mature way to move forward in a godly and God-centered relationship. Although I never touched another woman in all our time together, it took me way too long to give my whole heart to the woman of my dreams.

Dawn and I met in February of 1996. I remember the day I ran from the warehouse, out to meet at her car, at five o'clock. This was a Friday. I had fully intended to ask her for her phone number. As I ran out the door, I couldn't find the black Escort that she drove to work every day. It was gone. I was so disappointed but what I didn't know was that she had left early that day. I seen her there in the morning, but to my great sadness she was gone in the afternoon. I had to wait a whole weekend to get her number. That may have been the longest weekend ever recorded, at least for me.

On Monday, I ran through the same situation except the outcome was amazing. I met Dawn on February 19 at 5:02 p.m. in the parking lot. I asked for her number and she gave it to me. I couldn't have been happier! On the way to my second job, I was smiling from ear to ear, I couldn't believe that this beautiful young lady had given me her number, and I couldn't wait to call her. I did that night about nine o'clock and we spoke on the phone until almost midnight. I did the same for the next three nights, and on the fourth night, which was a Thursday, I went to her house right after work. I've never been more excited to spend time with any one person more than Dawn.

Dawn was living with her parents and her daughter. I spent time getting to know her daughter, Tori. While Tori and I hung out and played in the living room, Dawn was with her mother making food and keeping busy in the kitchen. I couldn't believe how right it felt; she had a daughter, I had a daughter. She had a true relationship with Jesus and I wanted to get back there. This all seemed more than perfect.

I stayed there for a couple of hours, and when it was time to go, Dawn stood with me in the entryway of her house. She had on gray leggings and a long beige sweater. Her hair was down, she had the most beautiful smile I've ever seen, and all I wanted to do was lean over and give her a kiss before I walked out the door that night. That was exactly what I did. As soon as I walked out the door, I skipped twice, jumped in the air, pumped my fist in the air, and thanked the Lord for the woman He brought into my life. Day one of the rest of my life. I lose my breath thinking about the way I felt that night and how I would feel so many times for the next twenty years. Although there were many times I felt frustrated, and I'm sure she did too, I love this woman with every bit of who I am.

Dawn and I each brought one child into our relationship. Our plan as we moved forward was to have more kids, how many we didn't know, and right off the bat we were going to wait a little bit.

We still had to get married, but a lot of things would happen between this time and our wedding.

But those who wait for Yahweh's grace will experience divine strength. They will rise up on soaring wings and will fly like eagles, run their race and not grow weary and walk through life and not give up.

—Isaiah 40:31 (Passion Translation)

Fighting Her Fight

Kathy had gone through a few different treatments. She had even had a bone replaced in her leg. We hoped that that would stop the cancer from spreading, but not long after the replacement surgery, they found cancer again in the same area. What happened next, I believed, would take the wind out of her sails: she had her leg amputated. She would have to learn to walk on a prosthetic leg, and in her weakened condition, that wouldn't be easy. I didn't go with her on the day she got her leg amputated. My sister Sue and my brother Ted were both there. I made a promise to myself that I would never miss another important time with Kathy, through the rest of her life. But as usual, I failed again. In the days after her amputation, I was there almost all the time. She was so brave, she talked like she was going to get around like every other normal person. I believe her with good reason: she worked hard. Just before Kathy had had her surgery, both Dawn and I had asked her to be in our wedding.

Through all this time my sister Kathy had been going through chemotherapy, I would get one hour for lunch. When lunch started, I would run to my car, drive the eighteen minutes from work to the University of Minnesota Hospital, spend twenty minutes with my sister, and then drive back to work. I did this every time she was in the hospital. I was and am thankful that my work chose to look the other way on my five to ten minutes of being late, just about every day. During this time, it seemed like all the time, but it was worth it, I was showing love to the person who so often through life had carried me.

As I did my daily routine this day, I ran to where she had physical therapy. Today she had on a prosthetic leg and I saw her for the first time trying to walk on it. She looked at the woman who was helping her and she pointed over to me and said, "This is my twin brother, the one who's getting married." She looked at me and said, "I am going to walk down the aisle at your wedding," and she did. On November 8, 1997, she walked down the aisle with our mutual friend, Bobby. Kathy was amazing, but her battle was not over.

In the fall of 1998, my sister Kathy was taking a turn for the worse. We thought her cancer was healed; we even went camping. She had had a couple of appointments with her doctor, where things looked good, but she started feeling less than 100 percent again. She went to the doctor again. He had done some different tests, and told her that the cancer had spread from her leg to her lungs. She had multiple nodules on both lungs, and her chances for complete recovery were growing slim.

And the God of all grace, who called you to His eternal glory in Christ, after you have suffered a little while, will Himself, restore you and make you strong, firm and steadfast.

—1 Peter 5:10

He's Stating My Case

Not much snow yet, but I know it's coming. It's Minnesota, it's the last week of December, and it's been fairly cold, just cold enough for my achy body to not want to bend. I loaded myself into my 2016 Kia Soul, one of the few things I still have after my separation. It's cool because I do need a car and I use it to make a little extra cash. It helps pay the bills and my lawyer. I wish things were different. I wish I wasn't driving around on Sunday night trying to make ends meet, but if I have to, I want God to ride with me, and He always does.

On this night I'm driving westbound on Highway 394. It's pretty quiet, when all of a sudden, my phone blows up. I'm getting a run about a mile down the road, somewhere near the Ridgedale Center. As I whip in through the maze that surrounds the mall, I figure out that my ride is not on this side of the mall, it's on the other side near the sports bar called Champs. I started to pull up toward the door when my phone rang; it was an Uber number, so I quickly answered the phone. The gentleman introduced himself as Eric. He told me he was about a hundred yards behind me in the parking lot. I turned my car around and headed back toward him.

There were only a few cars in the parking lot, and I saw man standing with both arms in his jacket pockets. When my lights flashed across his body an arm came out of his pocket and waved his cell phone at me. I knew this was my guy. I pulled up next to him and put the car in park. He grabbed the door handle, opened the door, and slid into my backseat. I looked up in my rearview mirror and asked, "Are you Eric?"

He said, "Yes, I am." I looked quickly at my phone. We were heading toward Eden Prairie, the time said twenty-three minutes till arrival. I asked Eric what brought him out on a cold night like tonight; he said that his mother was in the hospital. She had just had heart surgery.

"Wow," I said, "that's kind of scary. How is she doing?"

He said she was resting, the doctor said they would know more in the morning. I knew right then before Eric left my car I would ask him if I could pray for his mom. It's kind of what I've been doing lately. I found out that Eric's mother's name was Darlene.

"Beautiful name," I said. "I can't help but hear that name and think of the Led Zeppelin song, by the same name." He told me he wasn't familiar with that song. I waved my hand and said that it didn't really matter, but what did matter is that "God hears our petitions and He loves your mom." He looked at me and asked if I really believed that. I said, "Yes, with my whole heart." As much as I do believe that, my personal life with my wife and family were in shambles. Believing that God loves me and is going to help me, is all I had left to hold on to, there was no way I was going to let that go.

Eric told me that growing up, he had gone to church, but as he got older, he started to question whether God was real. And if He was real, did He really care for each one of us individually? It seemed impossible to Him. At that point, he claimed to be an atheist, an atheist with doubt. I gave him the look, the look when you are confused. Like a sudden change in wind direction, he started spitting out everything I was prepared to say.

His doubt began and ended with the human body. We are so intricate from the very start of our existence, we are built of millions and millions of cells that make up our DNA, and if one chromosome were even off by the slightest amount, it would mean no life at all. There's no way that we mutated from nothing. Eric was making this easy for me, he was building the argument for a perfect design or intelligent design, or God!

Gravity explains the motions of the planets, but it cannot explain who set the planets in motion.

—Isaac Newton

Facing the Facts

It's Tuesday, September 10, 2013. The kids and I are starting our first day of homeschooling for the year. We have most of our books, but not all of them. We always start our day with Bible reading, and we had just finished up when the phone rang. Micah ran and grabbed the phone; he had a couple of quick words with whomever it was on the phone and ran toward me. He said, "Dad, it's Kristi." Since we had just started school, I was prepared to tell Kristi, Dawn's best friend, we could talk more later, but instantly by the tone of her voice I knew something was wrong.

She asked me if I was alone; she said she had something to talk about. I told her I would go outside, went out, and sat at the table on our patio. It wasn't hot yet, but our umbrella had been left up from the day before. I could tell something serious was up, but I was not prepared for what I would be told in the next few minutes. She asked if I had spoken with Dawn. I replied that I had not. She then asked if I was sitting down, because she had something serious to tell me. Kristi told me about an incident that happened the day before.

Dawn's business partner, Jon, had been out sailing the day before with his wife and his sister and her husband. Jon had left his phone near his wife and had left. Julie, Jon's wife, picked up his phone and started looking at it. Jon had recently texted Dawn and said, "I miss you Babe." This floored Julie. This was something that she always thought was a possibility, and everybody, myself included, hung it over her head, like a ton of bricks. She instantly brought this to Jon's attention and she asked him what was going on and for how long it had it been happening. Eventually he admitted to having strong feelings for Dawn, and Dawn had feelings for him too. I couldn't believe what I was hearing. Dawn had always been the best person I had ever known. This couldn't be possible, my whole world was crushed. This wasn't possible...I started to sob. I told Kristi that I had to call Dawn and find out the truth. There had to be an explanation, one I could live with, because I couldn't live with what I was hearing now...

I called Dawn right away. I told her that Kristi called and told me about Dawn and Jon's relationship and the text that Julie found. I asked if this was true; she didn't answer me. I told her she had to talk to me, if she didn't talk to me now, I would come to her workplace. She, at that point, told me she would come home. That was the longest thirty minutes I can remember.

When she got home, she came up into our room and sat on the bed. I asked again, "Was this true?" She shook her head and sobbed. She said at this point, she didn't want to live anymore, that she had been living a double life. She would later say that the double life was not about her relationship with Jon but with me and whether she loved me or not. She always thought that I had an affair on her; I never did, although she accused me multiple times.

One time, a girl that I worked with at Dominoes asked for a ride home, she didn't have a way home. On the way there, I asked her how things were going. She said that she and her boyfriend, who is the father of her son, had been fighting. I asked her if I could pray for her and her boyfriend. She said yes. I put my hand on her shoulder and prayed for their situation for maybe one minute, then I went home. It was late. As I crawled into bed, Dawn asked me why I smelled like a woman. I told her, but she did not believe me and started accusing me of an inappropriate relationship. I couldn't say what happened enough times for Dawn to believe me. I'm not sure why at this particular time the enemy planted a seed; sometimes it takes years for that seed to grow. I told Dawn that I would never give the coworker a ride again, because I wanted to make Dawn happy, not because I had done anything wrong.

Anyone who truly knows me knows that I would pray with someone that I don't even know, in the grocery store. How much easier is it for me to pray with someone I do know? I can claim my innocence from now until eternity and it wouldn't matter to Dawn. What does matter is, I'm not claiming innocence to please her, I am claiming it because it's the truth and I have to stand before God. He's the only Judge that matters.

I have chosen the way of truth and faithfulness;
Your ordinances have I set before me.

—Psalm 119:30 (AMP)

Shop, Sweat, and Tears

It's the fourth day of the vacation from hell, yay, shopping day. There are thirteen of us and I know most of this day I'll be alone. To shop you gotta walk, and walking is an issue. Poor me.

I can't blame them; they are all here to shop, to enjoy a part of the world that they have never been to, I get it.

It's midmorning. We got out of the cars with the crowd of people who traveled with us, I mean family. They all dispersed in different directions. I rested my butt on a short wall, in the shade, across from a restaurant where I knew at some point I would go across the street and try to get some ice coffee. I generally don't like hot drinks, but I do love caffeine. I had quit drinking soda years ago due to my addiction to Mountain Dew, the best drink ever, but I was thinking about having one today. Mountain Dew is my friend, and unless I throw it in the garbage, it wouldn't leave me or ever forsake me. I've always used these words in a different context, but today I'm feeling snarky.

The sun was creeping across the street, my butt was sore, and the scenery in front of me and to the right and to the left of me had become extremely boring. I pushed myself up off the short wall and angled myself toward the restaurant across the street; the need to use the restroom was becoming my first thought.

It is the Lord who goes before you,
He will be with you; he will not leave you or
forsake you. Do not fear or be dismayed.

—Deuteronomy 31:8 (ESV)

Nothing at All

The joy of not having to say anything was very apparent just by my smile. My Uber God was doing all the talking through Eric and all I could do was smile. It's pretty awesome when God steps in and does it all for you. I wasn't ever going to change Eric's mind about his beliefs, but I didn't have to. God was working on him, and I wasn't given the opportunity to mess it up. It was actually very nice to not have to say anything, which is a little unusual for me because I really like to talk, probably too much sometimes. Thank You, Father for keeping my mouth shut and for doing everything that needed to be done.

Our trip was just about done. I rounded the corner and stopped in front of a beautiful house. I looked at Eric and said "Wow, you have been blessed."

He looked at me and said, "Yes, I have!"

Tonight I thought I would be praying for Darlene, and though I didn't pray for anyone, I saw God working on the mind and heart of someone in my car and I didn't have to say a word. Thank You, my Uber God.

> Then your innocent distractions
> Hit me so hard
> My emotional reaction

Caught me off guard
It was nothing at all (Ann and Nancy
Wilson, "Heart")

The Easy Step

Every part of everyday works in segments for me: I get out of bed, I use the restroom, I go back to my bed, I sit down, I get dressed, I walk downstairs, very slowly. If Dawn hasn't left yet, I make her tea, or food, or both, depending on how far she is into her morning routine. Nothing for me is fast.

In this moment it works the same way. I take one step after another, but my only thought right now is getting to the bathroom and getting there on time. I asked the hostess where the restroom was; she pointed toward the rear of the restaurant. A concerned look was on her face. She said, "It's a little tricky," and explained that it was down a skinny hallway and up one step, second door on the left. I started moving toward the restroom that I needed to be in right away, but she was right, it was tricky, and it was a long hallway. Although I did make it up the one big step with no issue, on the way back it wouldn't be an easy place to get through. Right now, I am happy that I am just moments from reaching my destination. I really gotta pee.

The room itself is probably 3×4 feet, not much room to do anything, other than what I had just finished doing.

I washed my hands in the tiny little sink. The whole room looked like it probably hadn't been cleaned in quite a while. I dried my hands and moved back so I could open the door. I moved out into the hallway and started heading toward the dining area. Five steps after leaving my new favorite pee spot, I could hear footsteps behind me. My first instinct was to move to one side so I can let the person by, but as I move to the left, the footsteps stopped. I turned and looked behind me; it was a waitress I had seen when I was up front. She had her phone in her hand and didn't look to be in any hurry. I told her it might be best for her to get by me because I didn't want to have to make her wait. She looked up, smiled, and started to move past. She quickly glided past me and with great ease she dismounted the treacherous step, without a worry in the world. Now it was my turn.

With some hesitation, I moved towards the step. On one side, I had nothing to hold on to, and on the other side was my lifeless arm. That did me little or no good in any situation that calls for strength, and my arms were not matching up with the obstacles in front of me. I was getting nervous, sometimes taking that next step brings fear and sometimes for good reason. It was time to press on…

I can do all things through Christ who strengthens me.

—Philippians 4:13

Forgiveness

Forgiveness is a very awkward and hard subject for me to deal with. I know that my healing depends on me forgiving others. In Matthew 6, it talks about how can God forgive you, if you won't forgive others. It's hard to forgive when you've given your whole heart, when you have been a good person, a good man, when you've changed your life because you wanted to please your wife. For me, being faithful and loving one woman was not initially easy, but it is what I wanted to do and what I did. The life I left behind meant nothing to me, no regrets. My family and my God were and are the most important part of my life.

I hate pulling out the onion analogy, but there are so many layers to forgiveness in my situation. I forgave my wife for what she had done. I wanted nothing more than for our relationship to resume and be cemented in Christ and His Word. But as we were trying to move forward, things continued to get worse. As I peeled another layer off our relationship onion, I had a very hard time with all the lying she did. She oftentimes left my home and went biking with Jon and would tell me she went somewhere else (like work). She told me things about Jon's divorce that were exactly the opposite of the truth. She gave reason after reason on why they both had to go on these work seminars together, even after they had been found out by me and others, that they were having a relationship. So many sleepless nights...

Loving with every part of you is exhausting; physically, emotionally, and even spiritually. Loving someone with everything you have can wear you out.

When that person rips your heart out, smashes your joy, and has no remorse, it makes you feel rejected and unwanted. The effects of betrayal roll over into all your relationships, with all your friends, family, and even your Uber God.

So many times, I lifted my hands and my heart to God and cried out, "Why is this happening, what did I do, and, God, what are You gonna do about it?" I want a quick fix, I want restoration.

I feel like I'm not the only one who has been hurt when God takes two and makes them one. There is pain on all sides, because of the ripping apart of divorce.

Physically there is a great feeling of loss. Loss of desire to move on, your motivation is crippled. There's a loss of your dreams for your family, for yourself, and for your marriage. They are gone. Sometimes, even your desire to live is shattered by the reality of love lost.

Emotionally, when your head and your heart never stop thinking about the love you lost, the pain is a constant reminder of what you will never have again. It's not like it was intended to be, not like God's plan originally was. The tears that fall from your eyes are like a slow-moving rainstorm that eventually stops dumping rain, but the heaviness of the atmosphere never goes away. It soaks you with sadness, because you're walking outside of God's will for your life. From your head to your heart, that drenching heaviness sucks your emotional well-being from your very soul.

Spiritually, the three-fold cord brought together in a marriage covenant hurts everyone when broken. Dawn, myself, and God, my Uber God, are all in a state of shock, embarrassment, and grief. Maybe for different reasons, but I know no one is more sad for the outcome of our marriage than God is. He gave us the playbook to get it right, and she chose to not use it. In different ways, I suppose I chose not to as well, but I'm not sure how...

For if you forgive other people when they sin against you, your heavenly Father will also forgive you. But if you do not forgive others their sins, then your Father will not forgive your sins.

—Matthew 6:14–15 (NIV)

Quick Trip Hits #1

I met a woman today. Her name is Victoria. I was instantly drawn because my second oldest is also named Victoria. The lady told me she and her husband are hoping to have a child soon. By coincidence, my Victoria was also hoping to have a child soon. At the end of our seven-minute drive, I was able to pray for her and her husband to conceive a wonderful, beautiful baby. I couldn't help but silently pray the same for my daughter as well. Thank You, Jesus.

Delight in the Lord and He will give
you the desires of your heart.

—Psalm 37:4

I picked up a gentleman named Hubert; he was from Houston. We bantered about the flood and about how he and his family were spared. We talked about his sister, who lost everything, and how she and her family's lives were saved by staying on a bed in the upstairs bedroom, while the water was rising in the room. Wow, so scary. By the time we got to the airport, I was fortunate enough to be able to pray with him, for him, and for his sister. Thank You for protecting and providing a way, when the world says there isn't one. You're a good, good Father.

> *...your Father knows the things you need,*
> *before you ask Him.*

—Matthew 6:8

The Walking Man #2

It's Sunday morning, midwinter 2007, and the day and the night before we were pummeled with a snowstorm. My neighbor had plowed part of our driveway, but the street hadn't been touched yet.

For many years at this point, my wife and I had taught Sunday school. I figured at least one of us should make it there. I asked the kids who wanted to go, and my daughter Bekah volunteered. And so, while everyone else stayed at home, Bekah and I jumped into our minivan and very slowly worked our way off our road and toward church. The roads were barely plowed and the sidewalks definitely were not. As we turned onto Stillwater Boulevard, I could instantly see my walker walking down the middle of the road, bundled up from head to toe and walking stick in hand. My first thought was *This guy is crazy*, but looking back on it now, I'm sure he was just watching. Bekah and I had just passed him and were about to take a right turn. In conditions like this, you never slow down, but today a car was coming and I had to stop. Starting again would be a problem. My tires spun in the deep snow and we gained no traction, to the point where I looked at Bekah and we both knew we weren't going anywhere. When all of a sudden, we were surrounded by six or seven guys in army fatigues. I rolled down my window, and there was a man with a full mask covering his face. He told me they were there to push us out. I couldn't hold back my smile; my Uber God had met me on a cold snowy morning in the form of mighty snow angels, who saved the day for my beautiful daughter and me. And the walker, he had a front row seat! It's funny how he just shows up.

Fight the Fire

Sunday nights are great at Revival, it seems like there is a newfound excitement in everybody there. The fire tunnel was in full rage, the smiles were plastered on the faces of every spiritual drunk who was dancing with the spiritual high that comes with not drinking anything but the Spirits of God. We were all staggering in the joy of the Lord, maybe kind of like they did in the second chapter of Acts. Wow, so much fun!

The rest of the night, I couldn't remove the smile from my face, or the joy from my heart, and I was ready to go share my Uber God with the rest of the world. When Revival ended, my night was just beginning.

I left Revival with a smile stretched across my face, from ear to ear. Tonight had been great! I was heading east on Highway 36 when my phone lit up with a run. I was eleven minutes from picking up the next contestant on "Who loves their Uber God?" I couldn't drive fast enough. As I got close to my destination, I had a pretty good idea I was heading toward Cowboy Jack's. It was only midnight, way too early to be closed, but tonight was a Sunday and maybe they give the cleaning crew a little extra time to clean up the puke and pee from this notorious party place. I pulled into the parking lot and that's exactly what it looked like. The parking lot was pretty bare, just a couple of cars and a couple ladies standing near the darkened front door.

As I pulled my Kia Soul around to the front of the bar, two ladies embraced in what I could tell was a slightly drunken state of friendship. The taller of the two turned and headed toward my car; she grabbed the handle of the back door and slid in. The light was on for just a moment, just long enough for me to look over my shoulder and see smudged makeup and puffy red eyes. She had been crying during her departing words with her friend. This looks like a good chance for my Uber God to step in and shine.

Our conversation started out simple with the exchanging of names, but the run of black goopy makeup under her eyes opened the door for heavier questions.

"You've been crying, are you OK?"

She replied that her marriage was falling apart and that she only wanted the perfect life for her two-and-a-half-year-old son, Blake. And she wanted nothing more than to reconcile with her husband, Andrew, but Andrew wasn't the same man she had married. As a matter of fact, they had switched roles. In the beginning he had been the one, in their relationship, who loved and relied on God; now all that had changed. The world and the party lifestyle had taken over where God once lived, and this young lady, who at one time wasn't living for God, now was.

Her name was Brianna. In many ways her name might as well have been Karl. Our stories are very similar: my wife had been the strong Christian in our relationship, but now I had grown stronger in my relationship with Christ. The enemy had weaseled his way into her life and she compromised the sanctity of our marriage. She no longer loved me. I knew exactly how Brianna felt. If I wore makeup, my eyes would have looked just like hers. I knew the pain she was feeling. In many ways, we wanted the exact same thing, and right at that moment, I knew exactly what to say, because I was living her nightmare. It was time to bring the Creator of the Universe into our conversation.

The prayer flew off my lips, like I had said that prayer a thousand times before, because I had. I prayed for reconciliation, I prayed that God would be glorified, I prayed that hearts would be turned toward God, I prayed for her child the same way I prayed for my own children, and for just a moment, I forgot she was in the car. This time with Brianna was as much for me as it was for her. My eyes were doing the same puffy, red, sore crying like-a-baby thing that she had done earlier, when I picked her up.

I can't believe that less than an hour ago, my heart was so filled with joy that it was ready to burst; now, I couldn't silence the sadness. My only comfort is in knowing that my Uber God has never left me and never will. I know He is the miracle maker and all things are possible through Him who gives me strength.

She started to leave my car and the light came on. Although her eyes were still stained with makeup, her incredible smile lit up my car, brighter than the dome light. She thanked me for the prayers, but looking back, I thank her and my God for the knowledge of knowing I am never alone. Uber God, bless Brianna…

The Lord is close to the broken-hearted and saves those who are crushed in spirit.

—Psalm 34:18

Divorce Care?

It's February 20. By 11 o'clock it has been a long terrible day, I can't say every part of it has been bad. I had a divorce care group and they are pretty solid group of nice people. We're not on the same page, which is fine, and I believe that's part of the reason I'm there. God tells us there are only two reasons that are permissible to get a divorce, that was our subject tonight. One of the reasons if someone has been in an adulterous relationship and they were the one who did not commit adultery. Then it is not a sin for that person to remarry. The other situation is where a believer marries an unbeliever and the unbeliever leaves her or him, that person is permitted to remarry again. But those are the only two reasons that it is permissible to remarry again without it being an adulterous relationship. These are not my rules, these are the rules of the Bible. God didn't tell us that marriage would be easy. He didn't say what society says—it's ok to say we just fell out of love. That is not a reason that God finds acceptable. Just about every Christian who gets married remembers the words of the pastor or priest that this covenant is not to be taken lightly, this is a very big deal to God, and we should treat it that way. There's no easy way out, and there shouldn't be. If people actually took it half as serious as God did, we would not have divorce in Christian marriage. God has very specific rules for marriage and the breaking of the marriage covenant and none of them are easy.

Half of the group or better, even the leaders fell on the side of it's a sin and God forgives our sins. I said it's not that easy. We might steal something God will forgive us; we kill and God forgives us we slander and God forgives us. None of these issues or sins come with a covenant that we make with someone else and God. We can't just choose that we don't like it anymore or it just doesn't work. We made a promise to our spouse and to God. That is the difference between everyday sins and sin of breaking our covenant with God and our spouse. Needless to say, I was not a popular person at our group tonight. One lady actually got up and left. Right or wrong sometimes the truth will convict you. We don't like to be confronted by our own sin. There shouldn't be an easy way out of a deal you made with God. It matters a lot to him; it also matters to us. After I said all of this, I did say that he died for all of us and loves us all very much. But that being said, he also said that we should obey him and follow his Word. I was the last person to speak tonight which is probably good. I sat there biting my tongue trying not to pop in at different times, because I believe I know just how important the marriage covenant is to God. There is no easy way to get out of your marriage.

It's a God thing but my night was a long-long way from being done. I texted back-and-forth a few times with a woman from the group. She's pretty young and has three young children. Most people who have met me or know me know that there's nothing more important to me than my wife and kids, functioning as a family. Most people think I am crazy wanting that with my wife. She at times has been the biggest pain in my butt and hurt my heart more than any person in my life, but she has given me hope, joy, stability and the love of a good Christian woman for many years. It was never better than when we were good.

With my sickness MS there can be confusion. She would often say if I truly loved her I would work harder at getting better. She didn't believe that MS is a disease that is almost always progressive. She believed I didn't have enough faith to be healed. But, I know I do have that kind of faith; and I am standing for it, knowing my God will come. I tried very hard to improve my health. For years I changed my diet; I quit drinking pop and eating junk food. I exercised on a fairly regular basis and never got better. She always thought I could do better and maybe in some ways I could have.

While I was a waiter at the Olive Garden I would walk a lot every day at work. I worked with a tray, carrying food. Even though I did this four days a week for up to 20 hours a week, I still was losing my ability to walk and use my right arm. Eventually I retrained myself to carry trays with my left hand and arm, not because I wanted to, but I had to in order to keep working. This allowed me to keep working for almost two more years. I wasn't getting weaker because I wanted to, the disease was starting to take control.

Hands Extended

I was trying to figure out the best way to attack this precarious step. Should I back up, should I turn around and go down backward, should I just sit down and cry? I didn't know what to do. As I stood there thinking about my situation, the waitress who had just passed me by was standing in front of me, with her hands extended toward me and asking me if she could help. I felt dumb. Sometimes, that one step to get you moving to a better place will be the hardest step of your day, and maybe your life. I took her arm as she helped me down the step. I hate being alone. Time to move forward. Today, my Uber God reached out His hands, in the form of a beautiful, young waitress, in a sleepy little shopping town, near Colorado Springs, just down the road from tomorrow's adventure, Pikes Peak. It's time to get high!

And your ears shall hear a word behind you,
saying, "This is the way, walk in it," when you
turn to the right or when you turn to the left.

—Isaiah 30:21

Uber God Everywhere

Seeing our Uber God at work isn't always in the car, and it shouldn't be, it should be wherever we are. Today, I went to Aldi to get water and food, to feed the homeless. While I was in the store, I ran into a gentleman who went by the name of Red. Funny, because his hair was not red. He helped me put two cases of water in my cart, we had a couple nice words, and he asked me about my limp. I told him about the disease they say I have (multiple sclerosis, MS) and why I was at Aldi; he told me about his hip replacement. Shortly after, while we were talking, his wife looked at him and asked him in kind of a stern voice, "What are you talking to him about?" He explained our conversation and went over to the next aisle with her. He must've told her more than what I heard because when I saw them both at the checkout, she sent me a "God Bless You," and a big smile as she pushed her cart into the next checkout line. Red offered to put the cases of water into my car, and he did it all with a smile on his face. I couldn't believe how awesome my Uber God was and is and will always be. We shook hands and Red went to his car.

As soon as I turned around, a Muslim woman, wearing a burqa, came walking up to me and asked me if I needed any help. I don't normally do this, but I instantly grabbed her hand and looked into her eyes, and told her that I appreciated her kindness, saying, "God bless you, ma'am." She smiled as I asked her what her name was. She said, "Miriam," and I smiled and said, "Like the sister of Moses." We were crossing barriers, barriers made by man and the enemy, to keep us apart and prevent us from seeing the love of Christ.

I told her that one day, I will be healed by Jesus, and I said, "I hope I see you again."

She responded, "I hope I see you again as well."

God is so good. Thank You for loving me, thank You for putting people around me who see You in me, and in what I do. Thank You, Jesus!

Do not neglect to show hospitality to strangers, for by doing this some have entertained angels without knowing it.

—Hebrews 13:2 (NASB)

Be My Strength

My hips are sore and my elbows are raw, pretty well carpet burned. I'm staring at the ceiling, feeling hopeless, mad, and incredibly unfunctional (I don't think that's even a word, but I think it fits). I feel somewhat pathetic considering my current state. It started just as I had made my last text to a friend from divorce care. I had a tickle in my nose and let out a huge sneeze. I don't have small sneezes anymore and this one threw me off the bed, where I was sitting, and onto the floor. I was a little stunned at what had just happened, but I wasn't worried about getting back up. Looking back, I guess I should have.

I crawled, or belly flopped, toward the bed and try to pull myself up. My legs would not bend, I couldn't get them under myself to push myself up. I tried over and over at the bed and at a chair and the chest at the end of the bed. This all started at 11:15 p.m. and at 2:30 a.m. I stopped trying. I lay under a chair and sobbed. I was embarrassed. My sister and brother-in-law were thirty seconds away; I didn't want to wake them up, but I probably should have. I didn't want to worry them, they have been more than kind by letting me stay in their house, in their basement. They were traveling soon and I didn't want them to worry about me while they were traveling in the next couple of weeks. I do have friends who would be here in a moment's notice, if I needed them, but tonight that would mean waking up Cheryl and Ric, and I didn't want that. I prayed over and over for God to give me the strength to pull myself up or give me the smarts to figure out a way to get off the floor. I slept for about an hour and started the process of getting up all over again. My elbows are now very raw, my hips are sore to where I can barely roll over.

How could this be God's plan for my life? I wanted to do so much more for the Kingdom, for my family, my wife, but here I am staring at a light, thinking if this is life and how I'm going to live, I don't want it. Now I'm back to sobbing and feeling sorry for myself. It's only an hour and ten minutes until Ric gets up to go teach school. I tell myself, I have got to get up and try with all my strength to pull myself up, but now I'm tired, I can't even try without going into pain. I figure that at least it's winter and no one will see my arms under my long-sleeved shirts.

At 7:15 a.m., I was able to pull the phone cord and get my phone. I made the call to their home phone. Lucky for me, Ric answered. He came downstairs right away and helped pick me up off the floor. He was already wearing his coat and hat and said he was walking out door. Thank You, Lord, for keeping Ric in the house long enough to get my sorry butt up off the floor. It was almost 7:30 a.m., I've been lying on the floor for eight hours; this personal hell felt like it lasted for days. "Please tell me, Lord, You have a better plan for me than the one I'm living now. Thank You."

I Will Always Love You (Part 1)

It's another blistering cold January night. I had just gotten back to my sister Kathy's house, after taking her son Derek to hockey practice at the Brooklyn Park hockey arena. He was not a finesse player, more of a tough guy playing a finesse position, a very physical skater with some scoring ability. I always enjoyed watching him play.

We came into the house and it was very quiet; downstairs, I could almost hear the TV. I figured that would be Erica, Kathy's daughter. As Derek and I came in, we split directions. He went down to Erica and I went up to see Kathy. As I approached Kathy's bedroom door, I could hear a scream from the basement: "Get your ice-cold hands off me, you jerk!" All I heard after that was Derek laughing hysterically. There's nothing like harassing your sister, or...loving them.

I lifted my hand and knocked on Kathy's door. I heard a light moan and a little noise as she told me to wait just a moment. I didn't mind waiting, tonight we had some stuff to talk about that I never wanted to talk about. Kathy and I knew that she did not have very long to live. We had been together since before day one. She had been my sleeping partner inside my mom, she had been stealing things from me ever since that time as well, like food. Kathy was my mom's largest baby, at almost eight pounds, and I was the smallest baby at just under six pounds. She didn't really steal from me, but I've always liked saying that. Together, we made it work in our limited amount of space. I'm just glad I was never alone.

Like I am now.

I sat down on the bed next to my best friend, my friend, who looked so different than most of our life together. I couldn't hold back the heartache I was feeling any longer, the tears were seeping from my eyes like drops from a water pipe ready to burst. She looked so different. Her hair, which had been very blonde and very straight her whole life, was now a little darker and short and curly. Why, I don't know. When she lost all her hair during chemotherapy, it grew back darker and curly, and although Kathy was never super skinny, the steroids that they had put her on had made her retain a lot of weight. On the outside, it didn't seem like it was her, and then she reached out, grabbed my arm, and planted a big wet kiss on me. I knew that on the inside, she was exactly the same and she was loving me the way she had done her whole life.

And the tears kept a-coming.

It took a few minutes to compose myself, to be able to look at her and talk. I held both her hands, stared at her eyes. I couldn't help but think when we were kids and we would harmonize songs together, it made me smile. Back in the '70s, Kraft marketed a product called Wrapple. It was a caramel apple, wrapped with a jingle that both Kathy and I knew very well, and we would harmonize the whole jingle; and why not tonight?

> Take an Apple... [linger]
> And a Wrapple... [linger]
> Eat it quick
> On a stick
> La da de da
> La da de da
> With Wrapples... [linger]
> From... [linger]
> *Crap!*

And then came the laughs! Just to see her smile, in all her sadness, meant the world to me and, I think, maybe to her as well. The next part of this night might be one of the hardest things I've ever had to do...

...the joy of the Lord is my strength.

—Nehemiah 8:10

Serving Up Hope

I just dropped someone off at the airport. I generally don't like waiting near the airport because there are thirty or forty drivers waiting for their next ride. I start moving toward Minneapolis, maybe five minutes down the road, when my phone tells me somebody needs a ride. I turn north on Cedar Avenue, heading toward Minneapolis. I'm two minutes from my pick-up.

I round the corner; my phone tells me my rider is right here. I'm not sure whether it's going to be a man or a woman because the name is Jordan, but within moments I see a young man waving his hand, letting me know he's my guy. I pull over and he jumps in.

I'm not sure what to think of this young man. It's not cold, but he's wearing a winter hat or beanie; he's kinda unkempt with a beard and mustache, not very thick. He is on his phone trying to coordinate something. I don't know what at this point, but by the end of our ride I have a much better idea.

I ask where he is off to. He replied, "To the north side." He was going to help a friend who was buying a new vehicle. He went on to say that this person was actually an employee of his, who was moving out of a homeless lifestyle. I instantly became curious because of how much I had worked with the homeless over the last ten years. Often, I have had different homeless people tell me they want to have jobs but no one would hire a homeless person. I had to find out what sort of business Jordan was involved in so I could tell my homeless friends.

I asked Jordan what type of business he was doing. He replied he was running a mobile catering service, where they did all the cooking and serving onsite, where all the work was totally done by homeless people, or formerly homeless people, and himself. He had been a chef and restaurant owner in the past, but wanted to do more. He wanted to incorporate what he knew with one of the problems facing society, homelessness.

He went on to talk about the problems he had been facing trying to rely on his workers, but then a smile crept across his face as he started to tell me a couple of examples of how people had been pulled out of homelessness. I started to tell him about my homeless ministry and asked him if I could share his name and number with a couple of people who I thought might make good employees. He gave me the thumbs-up, but asked that I make sure they are serious about working. Sometimes, they are a lot of work, and you become invested in them emotionally as well as financially. I said I would. He went on to tell me that if I wanted to know more, a local news outlet had just done a story on his nonprofit catering business. Ironically, the local news had just done a story on my homeless ministry and my struggles with my health. This conversation gave me an avenue to bring Christ into what we were talking about.

I told Jordan that, regardless of our circumstances, God can use us to do good in the lives of others and that He loves us all. At that point, I thanked him for helping the ones who feel hopeless and giving hope where it can't be seen. I pulled up to his destination, we exchanged a few words, numbers, and handshakes. As he started to leave, I asked if I could pray for him. With some reluctance he said OK. I thanked God for Jordan and asked him to bless the work he was doing with the homeless and to provide great health and joy that overflows. He was smiling a goofy smile as he left my car, like maybe now he has a better idea why he started this crazy adventure in the first place.

A couple of times I've encouraged some homeless friends to call Jordan and gave them his number, but nothing happened. And when I spoke to Jordan, he said he never heard from anyone. You can lead a horse to water, but you can't make him drink. In the same way, you can tell them how much they are loved by Jesus and what He did for us all on the cross, but you can't force salvation on them, they gotta want it. Sometimes it's hard to crawl out of that rut we all get stuck in; that's when we need our Uber God most.

And a voice from heaven said, "This is My Son,
whom I love, with Him I am well pleased."

—Matthew 3:17

Quick Trip Hits #2

I met a young lady at Muldoons Bar in White Bear Lake named Kayla. As I drove her home, out of the blue I said to her that God will lead us where He wants us to be and He is always good. I could feel the smile on her face, before she said a word. Then she said, "God is good!" And she went on to say that not that long ago, in her young life, God hadn't been a part of it. She had recently gone to a conference/seminar which brought to light her need for the Savior. The joy in her voice and the excitement for the life she is now living with Jesus was exciting and encouraging. I couldn't help but smile the whole time she was in my car. When I dropped her off, I was honored and blessed to pray blessings over Kayla and the rest of her life. God has great plans for her and she's going to do it. She loves my Uber God, and He loves her.

Rejoice in the Lord always [delight, take pleasure in Him]; again I will say, rejoice!

—Philippians 4:4 (Amplified)

Lu and Emily, I met them on a Thursday evening. They are quite an inspiration, being from China. While here in America, they became Christians, despite opposition from their parents. He said that he was a hard person to convince of Christianity, but God can overcome any ethnic and financial barrier, even when it looks that they had no need of God, having recently taken a position at Google. Being very well off and very well educated, they still realized their need for the Savior. He, who loves them, will never leave them and never forsake them; everything else is material. Their story of coming to Christ is inspiring. Lu and his wife are now expecting a baby, praise God for Lu and Emily!

For I am not ashamed of the gospel, for it is the power of God for salvation to everyone who believes, to the Jew first and also to the Greek.

—Romans 1:16

Lead Me On

It rained this morning and it was kind of crazy around my house. We are preparing for our first graduation party for our first of five children. Kalie, who is my oldest, is the only one not present. She lives with her mother on the other side of the city. Distance and separation are sadly a very true reality for our relationship. Unfortunately, Kalie hasn't always felt loved and appreciated in our home. There is some truth in how she's feeling, but there is also truth in the fact that she's a teenage girl.

It's forty-five minutes before guests start to arrive, and Kalie had just shown up. She was helping set up the food and drinks when our home phone rang. Micah, my baby, answered it and yelled, "Dad, it's Uncle Conrad!" I didn't feel like I had time to talk, and he was going to be here with my dad in just a short while. I grabbed the phone, almost irritated, when he gave me the news that our father had fallen down and that they would not be making it to the party. He was pretty sure that my dad had broken his hip. The first thought that crossed my mind was my father had taken his last steps.

My father had grown up in a very different environment than most. His mother, who was brought up in the Jewish faith, had met a young man and married him. He was a Catholic. Her whole life was changed in a very short period of time. In some ways, she was shunned by her own family. Esther Rosen and John Gertz married, and in three years had three sons. The oldest was John, and then Marvin, and then my father, Gordon. The joy that filled their home was short lived. Within thirty-five days of their last child's birth, the three young boys were left fatherless, their father had passed away from tuberculosis. Although they had all been baptized, they now had no one in their lives to point them toward the cross. But God always has a plan. That plan might take eighty-four years to come to fruition, and part of the plan may not even be born for forty-two years, but God doesn't deal with time issues the same way we do. A short or long period of time is irrelevant when you are talking about eternity.

The news came through later that day, that Grandpa Gordy had broken his hip. Surgery would happen early Monday morning. I knew I would be there because there was something we had to talk about—salvation, and whether he wanted it or not.

It was Monday morning, about 10:30 a.m. I was wandering through the halls at Hennepin County Medical Center trying to find his room and the right words to say; hoping I would find time to be alone with him. As luck would have it, or God would have it, all three of my wishes would come true. God is so good. My father never remarried after my parents were divorced, but he had a long-time girlfriend of more than thirty years and, to put it lightly, she was hard to deal with on many levels. She was just plain ol' mean, but my dad put up with her, the same way she put up with him. I know they loved each other, but honestly, I don't think they liked each other at all. It's not perfect, but it's better than being alone.

I walked into his room, excited that I was the only one there, and nervous about the way to proceed in our conversation. I walked toward his bed. His eyes were closed, the only noise was the oxygen respirator that was pumping air into his tired old lungs. The strong man I had admired throughout my youth was nowhere to be seen.

I leaned over his bed fighting back the tears, when out of the blue I heard his voice. "Hello, Karl." I looked up toward his face into his blue eyes, just like mine, only to see the smile that I was longing to see. His eyes were clear, clearer than I could ever remember. God was giving me these moments, and these moments might affect the rest of eternity.

I hugged and kissed my dad, just like he had taught me to do. My whole life, he had said never be ashamed to love the ones you love with your whole heart. I will never stop doing that. Thanks, Dad.

Our conversation started out simply. "How are you feeling? Have they told you anything about your surgery?" He had just woken up from his surgery and didn't know anything. I told him that I had some questions for him, and he replied to go ahead. I started out talking about his life. I pointed out that he had always honored both Jewish and Christian faiths. I talked about how, during worship, nobody sang louder, or had their hands higher, than him, when I had brought him to church. He said that was because he was such a good singer. He lay there with that silly Gordy Gertz look on his face that everyone who knew him knew.

My next question would be a little more difficult. I didn't want to sway or make decisions for him. I pointed out how the Old Testament always pointed toward Jesus Christ, and I asked my father if he believed that Jesus was the Son of

God. He replied without a moment of hesitation, that, "Yes, He was."

My next question was, "Do you want to spend eternity with the Father, Son, and Holy Spirit?"

He again answered without hesitation, "Yes, I do."

My heart was pounding as I asked him the last question. "Do you want to pray the salvation prayer with me?" He said yes again, without missing a beat. The words of our prayer were simple but hard for me to say, because I could not stop crying. I couldn't help but think of how my Uber God had stepped in, and had changed circumstances, so He could be glorified, and so that Gordy Gertz, His long-lost prodigal son, could have eternal life with Him.

My dad for years had been slowly losing his ability to think clearly, but today he seemed totally with it, maybe forty years younger than his aging mind and body were letting on. Thank You, my Uber God, for being my Superhero!

Changing the Atmosphere

March 17, 2018, St. Patrick's Day—God likes to change the atmosphere. He does it in different ways all of the time. Tonight while I'm out Ubering he definitely did it. I'm at University and Broadway. I just dropped someone off and I get a call to a pick up seven minutes away. I take a left and start driving west up and over the Mississippi River. I'm heading towards an area I know pretty well. One because I have a friend who owns a tire shop on one side of the road and bars on the other side, that maybe at one time I hung out at. Tonight I'm pretty sure my rider definitely wasn't going to get new tires so I took a left into a bar called BJ's. BJ's was and is a strip club. I parked outside the door and waited for my person to come out. It wasn't but a minute or two before he came outside with a friend. They got into my car and were a little loud; and they were obviously feeling pretty good. I smiled and said hello. I asked: "How was the bar tonight?" They said: "this bar is a lot like a VFW with girls taking their shirts off," and they were laughing.

I smiled and started to drive them home. They didn't seem like bad guys but they were rather vulgar, but not bad like others. I've had in the past. I asked if they had plans for tomorrow, they said to sleep in and then one of them asked me if I had plans. And that's when the car came alive with the presence of God. I told them that I ran a Sunday school program in south Minneapolis at Little Earth a Native American Community. The one gentleman was familiar with that area and started asking questions. And I started telling them how God has been working in that area through the kids, their families and other adults. They are investing their time and love for God into a community that needs a touch of God in their lives. The moment I brought up doing Sunday school and loving on the people of Little Earth the car went from a very brash and worldly atmosphere, to one filled with Uber love, from an Uber God. These guys genuinely seemed to care what God was doing in south Minneapolis. They asked questions and had thoughtful and heartfelt responses to things I had been saying. God changed the atmosphere in my car in less than a few minutes.

Oftentimes I feel like my rides are not successful unless I pray with them, but today God showed me that sometimes, maybe all of the time, it's always about showing his love to his people whether it's at a south Minneapolis reservation or a strip bar in North Minneapolis. God is always good. He loves all of his children and wants us to show his love wherever we go .

Changing the atmosphere. I think of the story of Elijah at Mount Caramel when he calls the people to come near. The people came even after they had been chastised. When he said who will you serve, Baal or the one true God of Israel? They came forward with expectation; they could smell the essence of God and it was good and something amazing was about to happen and it did.

God stepped up and defeated the prophets of Baall and the prophets of Asherah—850 total he sent down an all consuming fire that destroyed the works of the enemy for everyone to see.

From the moment Elijah called the people forward, the atmosphere was changed. The table was set and the people would see that through faith in God, that Satan and his minions didn't stand a chance. Sometimes just bringing the name of God, Jesus Christ, into your conversation will change the atmosphere. I know it did tonight. It is so cool serving an Uber God!

Playing Charades

For three and a half years, we played the game. The game that neither one of us was going to win.

I was Dad, she was Mom, we had three kids together, two we brought into our marriage, five in total; two dogs, two cats, and eight chickens. From the outside everybody thought we had it all together, even our Bible study that we both led, at different times through the years. They didn't know that we hadn't slept in the same room since August 10, 2013; that we never held hands, never kissed, that we never talked the way we once did.

She never shared her day-to-day feelings with me about our kids or each other. And we avoided the big elephant in the room, her work, and her relationship with her business partner, Jon, who started this whole fiasco. So many times arguments erupted about times and places they went together. I think back to other people's remarks about the two of them and how they seemed like husband and wife to everyone they met. The stories or occurrences were not from random people, but from family and close friends.

I remember begging my wife not to leave and go with Jon, on different business vacations. I called them vacations because, sadly, she took him where she and I had had special times together, like the ejection seat on top of the

Stratosphere Tower in Las Vegas; like the pink jeep ride in Sedona, Arizona. They had gone to sporting events and concerts on a regular basis, while we had spent only a couple of weeks alone together in our twenty years of marriage. She had done more of that with Jon, in just a few years. He had stolen my wife, but ultimately it's not stealing if somebody gives it to you.

It's hard to blame anyone except myself for not being a man. I should've taken the responsibility for my family and stopped what Dawn and Jon were doing. He's a selfish person, and Dawn is stubborn, and I was weak. Some of my weakness grew out of my own ignorance, and trying to believe that the things that were happening couldn't really be happening. I've always known Dawn to be a God-fearing woman. The relationship that she was carrying on with Jon didn't seem like one that feared God or worried about what was right. I'm guessing because I didn't know what she was thinking, but what I do know is that she didn't love me anymore.

The last time I heard her say those words, "I love you," was February 20, 2015.

I Will Always Love You (Part 2)

I wrote a song for Kathy that I was going to sing at her funeral, but I wanted her to hear it before then. I wanted her to hear it tonight. After I told her my intentions, she told me, "Come on, Karl, let's hear it." I closed my eyes and I held her hands tight, and fought back the urge to cry, then let out the words from my heart, not just from me but from everyone who had ever known Katheryn Elaine Gertz.

I Will Always Love You

March 31 in 67
Until the day you went to heaven
Hand in hand, through the years
Through the laughter and through the tears

(Chorus)
And I will always love you
Everything that you stood for
Everything that is good
And my love will always be true
Oh, my sister, I love you

UBER GOD

Your sexy smile, your silly ways
The way you brightened up every day
You made them happy, you made them sad
You were always cherished by your mom
and dad

(Chorus)
And they will always love you
Everything that you stood for
Everything that is good
And their love will always be true
Oh, our daughter, we love you

One little boy, one little girl
You were number one in your world
She loved you, Bobby, for half your life
He loved her too, he made her his wife

(Chorus)
And they will always love you
Everything that you stood for
Everything that is good
And their love will always be true
Oh, our mommy, we love you

We love you Kathy, we raise a glass
The way you fought your cancer
You did it all with class
Our love for you will never end,
We toast your honor
Because we're your friends
And we will always love you,

Everything that you stood for
Everything that is good
And our love will always be true
Oh, our friend, we love you
And our love will always be true

Oh, my mama, my daughter, my auntie,
my friend,
Oh, my sister, we love you
Whoa...

I lost where I was, but I always knew who I was with. I was with my best friend and I was being lifted up by my Uber God. He gives me strength, when I don't have any.

He gives me words, when mine are few.

And He gives me love, even when I don't deserve it.

God, You are good!

Kathy died February 9, 1999. Less than a month after I sang these words to her, I sang them at her funeral. I can't wait to see her again.

Getting High

It's been a long time since I got high, but today I was going to get high regardless of how low I felt. We were taking the cog rail to the top of Pikes Peak, all 14,114 feet of her. Our trip to Colorado was heading toward the end, and so was my marriage to the love of my life, who I felt couldn't care less.

We started the trip by boarding the cog rail at the mountain base. Basically, the cog rail is a glorified train which slowly takes you up the drastic incline of Pikes Peak, one cog at a time. It's a fairly sunny day, the temperature is in the low 80s, as we venture onto our mountain transportation. We all get to sit fairly close to one another, but all three cars of the cog rail are pretty full. My children, Rebekah, Isaiah, and their cousin, Brooke, are sitting across from Grandma and Grandpa. In our section, my other son, Micah, is in between Dawn and I, and across from us are, our other daughter, Tori, and her husband, Shawn. Rachel (Dawn's sister) and her husband, Jimmy, are sitting with their kids Judah and Shaina in another section. The car is quiet. This is going to be a long ride to the top of the mountain.

I think how the enemy has strongholds over our lives over cities and regions; maybe with our altitude today, we would be higher than him and his demons. So, I think to myself, I know there is nothing bigger than my God. As we climb the mountain, I wonder what the chances are of saving our relationship. Our marriage was slowly fading away. My head was literally in the clouds. I need my Uber God and I need Him uber fast. The peak is in sight, but soon it will all be downhill, and it's hard to stop a rolling stone.

Tortured

In the weeks that followed the unveiling of the truth, everything was such a blur. Dawn was working late almost every night; she told me she was having a breakdown. Her business partner, Jon, was there to console her. On the weekends, she was generally home on Saturdays, but every Sunday, she would take off, not letting any of us know where she was going on her bike. She would meet up with Jon, somewhere, and not come home for five or six hours.

This, in many ways, was like torture, not knowing where they went or what they were doing. She barely spoke to me for weeks. On different occasions, I had asked her what her plans were, what was she going to do? She told me that if she had to make that decision right then, I would not like the answer. I felt that she was going to leave me very soon, like yesterday; sadly, she wasn't just neglecting her duties as a wife but she also wasn't paying any attention to the kids. They were my responsibility, and she knew that I would take care of them.

We oftentimes had dinner with Dawn's parents, on Wednesday nights. After weeks of Dawn disappearing on Sundays, and sometimes Wednesdays, like this night, I brought up to her parents what had been happening. I felt like she was phasing me out. I asked if they thought I should talk to a lawyer; they didn't think that I should, but out of this conversation an idea was birthed in her family that I wanted to take Dawn for everything she had. Nothing was farther from the truth. This was late October 2013, and this was just the beginning of almost four years of sadness and betrayal. There was nothing more I wanted than to be in a loving relationship with my wife. There had never been a better time in my life than the time I spent with Dawn, when things were good. She had been the best person I had ever known. I still wanted her to be my one and only.

> And I fell for you,
> no more lonely,
> one and only,
> yes, I fell for you

—Karl Gertz

The Walking Man #3

I'm standing by the front door waiting for a young friend of mine to arrive; his name is Winter. It's a pretty cool day, but at least it's sunny. He appears to be running a little late.

On this night, we are filming my wife and a friend of ours speak on the freeing power of Jesus and how we should leave our hurts and our burdens at the foot of the cross. She was giving her testimony on her deliverance and she asked if I knew anyone who could film it, and I knew Winter.

Winter showed up and he put his equipment in my minivan. I felt a little rushed and I started barreling in reverse down the driveway. I looked in my mirror to see someone standing at the end of my driveway. I locked up my brakes. It was my walker right behind my car. He had no reaction, like I hadn't startled him, like I had startled myself. He pulled his hat down and pushed through the snow with just a slight nod of his head, his one-piece Carhartts and his Blaze Orange hunting hat and warm gloves would protect his body from the outside elements, but the big stick in his right hand would help him maneuver through the icy terrain. Regardless of the weather, my walker was more dependable than a mailman. Him just showing up in weird circumstances makes me feel like he's got his eye on the situation. But who knows?

When Your Joy Comes!

It's early spring and it's a bright day, but not too warm. I'm in downtown Saint Paul picking up, around ten in the morning. I'm not really thinking about my Uber God, but I am always happy when He jumps in my car, and He did, with my two passengers Jenny and Mike.

We exchanged names and had a few pleasantries, and then they slipped into their own conversation. I started eavesdropping only because that's my job, and I wanted to.

I sensed trouble from the very beginning. She was from Boston and he was from New York, sports rivals. One loved the Yankees and the other was a huge Bo Socks fan. I'm surprised they were sitting next to each other. She had been here for at least a week down at the Mayo Clinic in Rochester, and he had just come in to town. At this point, I couldn't quite figure out why they were here, but I decided if I kept my mouth shut, they might let me in on their reason for being in the Twin Cities.

Mike was holding her hand when he leaned over and asked her, "How are you feeling?"

Jenny said, "Not too bad, but it could get worse later." Questions started running through my head but I kept my mouth shut, which is hard for a big mouth like me.

Jenny told Mike that her treatments had started on Tuesday and she was done on Thursday. She was surprised on how well she felt and that she was actually hungry and couldn't wait to get to the restaurant, down near Loring Park, Eggy's. Jenny said, "The reviews and the pictures looked amazing."

Too many bits of information for me to stay quiet any longer. I had to ease into their conversation and I only have a couple of minutes. I asked how in the world did a Yankees fan and a Red Sox fan ever put up with one another. They both started to laugh, and Mike said, "We don't," which made them laugh even harder. I told them I had heard great things about the restaurant they were going to and that it is somewhat famous in certain breakfast connoisseur circles. And I assured them that I wasn't in that circle.

We pulled up in front of the restaurant, I looked back at Jenny and said, "I overheard about some of your health issues. Would it be OK to pray a blessing over you?" She held her hand up to her mouth with a small gasp, nodded her head, yes. I thanked the Lord for Jenny and Mike, I prayed for good health on both of them. I prayed that any joy that had been stolen would be replaced ten times over. I could see a tear in the corner of her eye. As I prayed that God would bless the Yankees and the Red Sox, the smile that had been there earlier was back. She thanked me with a big smile, as both she and Mike scooted out the right side of the car. Thank You, Lord, for giving me the opportunity to spread your joy and your love! My Uber God is oh so good! Thanks for sharing!

Take Me to the Top

Being on the top of the mountain can be very lonely and cold. In the last ten minutes, the terrain had been void of any life at all; the skies had turned gray and snow was lightly falling. What a contrast to what it used to be, way back in the beginning of our journey.

There is great sadness at being on top, because from this vantage point you can see the good times behind you and all the accomplishments along the way. And how they are slowly rolling away. I hate reflecting on the past, but the reality of my current situation is I'm sitting on a train, 14,000 feet above sea level, all alone, as all my family are taking in the heights and sights of Pikes Peak. In this moment, I can see and feel my past, and what my future looks like. Life sucks!

The chill of my reality blows like a cold mountain wind that scares the crap out of me. Oops, it's time to go change. But it only gets worse, until the healing begins, 'cause even mountains have valleys.

Even though I walk through the valley of the shadow
of death, I will fear no evil, for You are with me...

—Psalms 23:4

Changing Directions

Sometimes, when you are driving for a transportation service company, things get a bit crazy busy in a hurry, but usually not on a Friday morning before 11:00 a.m. I always appreciate keeping busy and I had just left my couple near the Loring Park area when my phone lit up. I'm heading toward Second Avenue and Fourth Street. I was picking up a man named Josh when I rounded the corner and realized I was in front of the Minneapolis Police Department. I instantly saw a young man standing near the curb, slowly waving his hand. He was nicely dressed but it looked like, maybe, he had been wearing those clothes all night. He had on gray slacks, dress shoes, and a purple shirt with a tie that matched, but the tie was worn very loosely. The purple reminded me of the Bachman's floral company.

He slowly got in the front seat and he looked very tired. My first thought was, perhaps Thursday had been a wild and crazy night, but those thoughts wouldn't stick around long. We exchanged names, and then I asked if everything was all right. He said, "Not anymore." He told me the night before, his sister had gotten married in a hotel near downtown. It was a fun, small event with just family and a few friends. After the wedding they went out to eat as a group, and he had had a few cocktails, maybe four. Just after he dropped off his girlfriend in the uptown area, he got pulled over. He thought for sure he would be fine, but soon after the officer had him blow into the breathalyzer, he was being escorted to the backseat of one of Minneapolis' finest, and his car was impounded.

Josh said he had blown a .11, but he was certain that he was fine. Now he was certain that this would affect every part of his life. I told Josh about my own encounter with the police twenty-three years earlier; I too had received a DWI but I knew for certain that I was drunk. That wasn't my point, my point was that sometimes we make bad decisions and God takes our bad decisions and puts us in a place where we can become better people.

We can show the love of Christ because of our experiences. The best things that happened in my life came out of that terrible circumstance. Four of my five kids were a result of me having to take a different job to change directions in life. I would never have gone in the direction I went, if it were not for the leading of Christ in my life after I had made bad decisions. Then I told Josh that God had an amazing plan for the rest of his life and beyond; things might get harder but let Him lead you.

He was very quiet as we pulled up to the impound lot. I asked if I could pray a quick blessing on him, and he nodded, "Yes," and I prayed, "Father God, please lead my brother Josh where You want him to be. I pray that the consequences that are ahead of him would be just and fair and fill him with hope for a better day tomorrow and for the rest of his life, thank You, Father."

I prayed this for Josh. But I was thinking about myself and what I needed back in the day; especially when I seemed to be too busy trying to screw things up to pay attention to You. You are my amazing Uber God…

The Prayer of Jonah

From inside the fish, Jonah prayed to the Lord his God. He said, "In my distress, I called to the Lord and He answered me, from deep in the realm of the dead, I called for help and You listened to my cry. You hurled me into the depths, into the very heart of the seas, and the currents swirled about me; all your waves and breakers swept over me. I said, 'I have been banished from Your sight, yet I will look again towards Your Holy temple. The engulfing waters threatened me, the deep surrounded me, seaweed was wrapped around my head. To the roots of the mountains, I sank down; the earth beneath barred me in forever. But You, Lord my God, brought my life up from the pit.'" (Jonah 2:1–6)

Out of the Blue

It's the first warm day of 2018, April 22. For nine months I have lived without my family, there have been times where I have done nothing but weep. It's a Sunday night, I spent the evening at revival. It was a great night. I had the honor of praying for a man named Brent. I could relate with Brent because I struggle walking and he has a tough time just standing up. I know God wants to heal us both but that's not where the similarities end. Brent and his wife had divorced. I don't know why but I could tell it still hurts him. He also has five children, just like I do. It kills a dad to not be with his kids. I look at my friend Brent in a wheelchair, and think to myself how far am I from his exact situation?

They handed me a microphone and asked me to pray for him. The words that came to my mouth for him were uplifting and encouraging. and I felt like there was a pretty good chance some of it may have been from pastor Doug Stanton, who had been preaching. But honestly, I believe it was the Holy Spirit speaking through me proclaiming the goodness and love of our Savior and how God the Father never planned for his children to be sick or disabled.

One night earlier was a very different situation. I was tired, not feeling great, but not feeling bad either. I had gone up for worship and was just moving back to my seat.

I grabbed my phone and took a quick peek to see if anyone tried to contact me. I was taken aback by the name of Julie. She was the wife of the man who my wife had had a relationship with. Besides that, Julie had been my friend in our Bible study for many years. My wife and I were also their youngest daughter's godparents. Wow this is getting messy... welcome to Jerry Springer—the Minnesota edition! My head and my heart filled with anger, at myself and anger with my wife. I was angry at myself because I had treated Julie terribly. I avoided her in many obvious ways: phone calls, texts and even going out of my way to make sure I didn't meet up face to face. I can only blame myself. But I did it to keep peace in my home and just keep a small chance of restoration to our broken marriage.

But now as I'm sitting in church when I should be excited and happy I am feeling just the opposite—sad and angry. If I were a power tool I would be spitting nails and sinking them all deep into cement. I'm not going to blame my wife for the way I treated Julie. But I only did it for one reason. I wanted the love of my life to love me back. I am mad because she never did. I am hurt because she never did. I've been an emotional wreck because she never did.

The transforming love of God is changing me almost daily. As much as my heart was hurt, my heart wants to reach out to others like Brent. We live in a world of brokenness. I feel as if we could gather a group of people from anywhere and find brokenness from heartache, to illness, and death. The enemy is working his plan to seek kill and destroy. I'm just glad that we know at the end of it all who wins. Thank you Jesus, my Uber God!

Coming Down

The change for me came years ago, when I decided to live my life for someone and some things other than myself. I changed from a self-centered, egotistical, only-thinking-of-me jerk, to someone who loves God, loves his family, and would sacrifice anything for either of them. Now the rubber hits the road, or the wheel scrapes the steel on our slow descent down the mountain.

It's only a few minutes and I see the first evidence of life. It's not much, and I can't tell whether it's a tree or a shrub, but I can tell it's alive. Within moments, there is more life sprouting everywhere. As we come down from this mountaintop experience the trees become vibrant with color and thick with life; as we descend a little lower, into an atmosphere that sustains life and doesn't choke it, I feel for the first time in a long time that I can breathe.

As we wait for another train that was dealing with a small fire, I looked deep into the lush beauty of this treacherous mountainside and I saw a big doe walking slowly toward me. I couldn't help but think about how my Uber God had saved my life through the beauty of His creation before and told me to press on, and does that mean anything now? The ride down is almost complete, but the road less traveled is the one we take home tomorrow. I am not looking forward to tomorrow.

Father God, bring forth new life, restore these dry bones, all in the name of my Uber God. Amen.

I will take joy in the God of my salvation. God, the Lord, is my strength; He makes my feet like the deer's; He makes me tread on my high places.

—Habakkuk 3:19

Life in Another World

I t's been a fairly busy night, or at least it seems busy. I've been working downtown, or Northeast Minneapolis, for the last couple of hours, lots of short rides. I am moving toward a pick-up near Broadway and University, I'm guessing at a bar, because there are a lot of bars right in that area, and sure enough, I was right.

I was picking up a woman named Claire. I waited out front for a few minutes when a young lady came up to my window and asked if this was the ride for Claire. I said, "Yes," with a smile. She then opened the door and said her wife would be out in a minute. I had to stop and think about it for just a moment. I said, "No worries," and asked, "How was your night?" She told me it had been a tough couple of days, that her wife's dog of seven years had just died the night before, somewhat out of the blue. Sampson (the dog) had seemed to be fine most of the day but hadn't eaten much, and as the day went on, he became lethargic and wouldn't play, which wasn't like him. They brought him to an emergency vet, where, while they were there, he passed away, and as much as they wanted to know what had taken the dog's life, they could not afford to pay for an autopsy.

At this point, I said, "I'm very sorry, Claire," and she said, "I am not Claire, I'm Rae." Just at that moment, the door opened and Claire poked her head in. She told us she had spoken with someone while she was checking out who had puppies for sale and wanted to check them out. And by a weird coincidence, they were Chihuahuas, just like Sampson.

I started to drive our short eight-minute ride together, and when we got to their house, I looked over at Claire. I could see a deep-seated sadness being covered by a delicate smile. You could almost feel the pain of losing someone or something you love in her eyes. It was my turn to bring comfort and the love of Christ into our conversation. I told Claire that "God cares about all of our hurts and He knows how much you loved Sampson, and He wants you to know how much more He loves you." The sadness that was in Claire's eyes was now seeping in a slow drip from the corners of her eyes; she was being touched by the hand of God. I asked if I could pray for her and she said, "Yes."

I prayed that she would find comfort in her Creator; that joy would be replaced over and over; that she would feel the love of God immediately; that their relationship would become real; and that the search for a new furry companion would be easy.

Claire thanked me for my kindness over and over. I felt like perhaps people who profess the name of Jesus may not have always shown love (to her) and she was thankful tonight that someone had. Rae had been very quiet since Claire got in the car, but touched my hand for just a moment as they both got out of the car. Her words were few as she looked up and said quietly, "Thank you!" My Uber God loves all of His kids!

Then Jesus stood up again and said to the woman,
"Where are your accusers? Didn't even
one of them condemn you?"

—John 8:10

Bring It on Home

It's our last day, the drive home. There was a part of me that wanted to stay longer and try to talk things out, maybe seek out a plan to save our marriage. I had seen different situations where God steps in at the last second and saves the day. Today that was my prayer. When Moses led the Israelites from Egypt and they were trapped against the Red Sea and God had a plan, He stepped in and saved His people. Damn it, it's my turn, I'm one of Your people, save me, save my family, save my marriage.

The rest of the family was up and out earlier than Dawn, me, and our two boys. Getting out early had always been part of her family's mind-set, but not ours. I could've left early or at the very least been ready to leave early because I didn't sleep much. I packed all my stuff and lay in bed, dressed and ready to get up and leave. I was silently praying for sudden revelation, for an answer to my messed-up situation.

The drive back to Saint Paul would be fourteen to fifteen hours. I wondered how the conversation would go. But that would not matter, because there was little or no speaking of any kind. We stopped near Omaha, Nebraska, at Panera Bread. It was an easy, lighthearted lunch, but soon we were gassed up and back on the road again.

Hear the cry of my heart...

I've seen You move, come move the
   mountains,
and I believe I'll see You do it again.
You made a way, where there was no way,
and I believe, I'll see You do it again...
(Elevation Worship, "Do It Again")

Not Alone

I have been humbled to the point of shaking my head. I have had so many great people helping me walk through the worst part of my life. From my friends Brian and Christine, Tim and Leslie, Kevin, Kevin (yes, two of them), John, Pete, Anthony, Linda, and Paul, to both my sisters and their husbands, my brothers and their families, and so many others. Every one of you have helped me in so many ways, you've given me hope when I didn't have any. You have given me food, even when I didn't want to eat. You gave me your strength when I had no strength or desire to carry on. You put clothes on my back, you have put gas in my car, and financially you have paid for things I had no idea how I could pay for, and you have given me prayers, when I was with you and when I was not.

Every one of you has given me a shoulder to cry on, a hand to hold, and an ear to listen. I know you all know my story. If you have been around me at all, you have heard it too many times. God has done so many things for me, through you, I can't thank you enough for your love and support. This is where so many of the verses from the Bible become true for me: "Never will I leave you, never will I forsake you." I have felt very lonely at times, but I've never been alone. We are called the body of Christ, we all have different purposes and giftings. Some of you folks walk with your hands wide open, some with eyes that see past a broken heart or a crippled body, some with big feet (Brian) to take big steps that move me in a direction toward God. God doesn't need us to make the miraculous happen, but He does love when we make the choice to serve Him.

It's never hard to see my Uber God in my friends and family... God, You are good.

And when did we see you sick and in prison and visit you?
And the King will answer them,
"Truly, I say to you, as you did it to one of the
least of these my brothers, you did it to me."

—Matthew 25:39–40

The Road to Nowhere

There was a little small talk, but not much, and the boys were quiet, maybe sleeping or watching a movie with earphones on, I'm not sure. Dawn interrupted the emptiness of the car with words she knew would drain my soul. She told me to enroll Micah at North Heights Lutheran School. At that very moment, I could see and feel the walls of my life and my marriage crashing down on me. "Hey," I started to protest. She had known that just days before we left on our trip, I had signed Micah up at our homeschool co-op where I had been on the board for six years, and was planning to be on for one more. I knew this argument would fall on deaf ears, her mind was made up.

Had she been holding back her intentions the whole trip? It's no wonder she treated me with disdain throughout the whole trip. While I was thinking of ways to reconcile our marriage, was she thinking of ways to end it? Uber God, You're late, hurry up, I need You!

Maybe He wasn't late, maybe it was time. The love of my life no longer loved me, maybe it was time to switch the love of my life from Dawn to my Lord and Savior, Jesus Christ. I needed to love the only One who gave everything for me. I needed to put Him first, but that wouldn't be easy, and neither would the next seven-and-a-half hours. Now, I just want the trip to be done.

"All I can say is…love stinks…"

(The J Geils Band).

Let It Be Done

It's Thursday, June 28, 2018. There is more heartache today than I've had in my heart in a long time. I open my eyes and looked for the clock. It was 5:55 a.m., time to get up. I pulled my broken body from the bed and gimped my way to the bathroom. I did all the things I needed to do to shower and shave and whatever else you need to do that starts with *s*, and got ready for a day I have long been losing sleep over. Today was the day to finalize my divorce, silence the screams, fill the void, wrap a tourniquet around my broken heart, and throw away the proverbial key. It was time to take steps in His direction.

I was the first one there. Our mediation was to start at nine o'clock. I wheeled my way onto the fourteenth floor before the clock struck 8:30 a.m., too much time to sit and think, but that's all I could do.

My lawyer showed up at 8:45. She started with some small talk about what to expect from Dawn and her lawyer. They didn't show up until ten minutes after nine. I couldn't help think about the facts. I was paying the mediator for his time, but they weren't even there. I'm frustrated. It's time to hit the app. I need direction.

The Lord directs the steps of the godly.
He delights in every detail of their lives.
Though they stumble, they will never fall,
for the Lord holds them by the hand.

—Psalm 37:23–24

Parents Dying Twice

Having your parents die is heart-wrenching. Having four parents die, that, to many, can seem inconceivable, but it's been my reality. My father died in July 2009, and my mother passed away in April 2015. I miss them both. They were both great in their own ways but struggled with their own sin and failures. Despite my parents' shortcomings, I chose to forgive and love them—like the example Jesus showed us.

Often, I put my wife's family and her parents before my own. I truly enjoyed being with them on a regular basis. The good things I saw in them, I didn't see in my own parents or in my upbringing. I admired the way my father-in-law was a provider and a leader for his family. In many ways, I wanted to be like him. And my mother-in-law had a love for the Father and a desire to go deeper in her faith that I appreciated more than she will ever know. She loved loving on her children and grandchildren. They were both generally always there for them and still are, but not for me. I wasn't flesh and blood, neither was my oldest daughter, Kalie (from an earlier relationship), but they loved her regardless of whether their daughter and I were married, and I truly appreciate that.

It would be foolish of me to say I don't get it. Their son had gone through a divorce where both he and his ex-wife had been unfaithful. He moved out of the house and moved to Texas and hardly ever saw his children. The job he had taken wasn't creating income to support his kids and for years he had little or no interaction with them or his family.

My in-laws, being wonderful grandparents, wanted to spend time with their grandchildren, and the only way to do that was to spend some time with their mother as well. She was doing everything on her own and not doing a very good job either, but she was doing the best she could. Their own son said that as long as they were involved in his ex-wife's life, he would not be involved in theirs, and he wasn't for years. This destroyed the perfect picture of the perfect life they had for their family and it was the precursor of what would happen years later when their daughter made decisions that would destroy her own marriage. They had learned the first time around when they had lost their son and didn't want to lose a daughter as well.

I don't know whether I would expect anything different. They accused me of planning to do things that had happened before in their son's divorce, like credit card fraud, stealing money, and not being a good parent. I don't know that anything I had ever done warranted that type of treatment. They knew the whole truth about their daughter's relationship with her business partner and somehow believed that I, too, had indiscretions with someone else. I never did and I would be willing to stand in front of anyone and bring forth witnesses to the truth.

All I ever wanted was reconciliation for our marriage. I forgave her and waited for four years, feeling despised because I never stopped loving her, I wouldn't stop, I couldn't stop. I was very sad when both my parents died, but when it was done, there was no more heartache and no more pain. But, with my in-laws, the hurt never goes away. They won't even look at me. It tears my heart out knowing that people I love and admire could care less about me. I understand the reason why; it doesn't mean it hurts any less. In the end I know where I stand in the presence of God and where the truth is, but right now, I only feel the pain of lost love. I need my Uber God. Please, Father, take away my pain!

Goodbye

We spent the next two hours throwing numbers back and forth. All I could think about the whole time was: "How am I glorifying God through this whole process of our divorce?" I'm sure it's making Him sick. This was a vow, a covenant made with Him and both of us. He was not being glorified by our divorce, but now I would try to glorify Him in how I acted toward the judge, the lawyers, and Dawn.

It's after 1:30 p.m., the mediator has left, and we aren't getting much closer to a compromise that would silence our marriage forever. The numbers going back and forth are being changed in twenty-five-dollar increments, frustrating, I'm sure, for both of us. We hit a point where I didn't feel like things would move anymore. My prayer for a long time has been, "Thank You, God, for being my provider. I want to glorify You." I knew that it was time to pull the trigger and put this behind me, the lies, deceit, and the heartache that had ruled my life for way too long. It was time to say goodbye.

Within minutes we were sitting in front of the judge, our lawyers had asked us both questions, and then the judge came back to me and asked me if I understood everything that was happening. I nodded my head, yes, and then I told the judge that God is my provider. She looked at me with an odd look on her face and said, "What?" and I repeated it again, "God is my provider."

She said, "He hasn't been providing for too many people around here." I looked away, back toward Dawn, and I felt this terrible feeling deep inside, that hissed like a serpent saying, "Thissss is over" (*The enemy comes to steal, kill, and destroy*, John 10:10). My marriage was done. I started to cry, the words going around the courtroom were just a smear of marbles in the mouth of a monkey, I didn't really understand or hear anything as I wept uncontrollably.

As I started to come back, I heard a dismissal of the courtroom. Out of the corner of my eye, I saw the love of my life start to stand. I pushed myself to my feet and looked her straight in the eyes and told her that I had always loved her and I still do. All these words came from me while I was sobbing in severe sadness over our love lost. How did we get here? She never wet an eye. And she hadn't cried once over us in years, why start now? I need my Uber God.

As I left the courthouse, with broken dreams and a broken heart, I couldn't help but think of my future, of all the things I would miss out on as a husband and a father. Life would never be the same and maybe that's not a bad thing, considering where we are now.

Quick Trip Hits #3

I t's late on a Saturday night. I'm in Eden Prairie thinking it's about time to end my night. When all of a sudden, my app goes off. I'm picking up Anna, who is just a few minutes away. She gets into the car carrying a kind of joy I only find in fellow believers. I asked her, "What has you out this late tonight?"

She replied, "I was with my family and we had been at the hospital with my ninety-two-year-old Christian grandmother who is in a coma."

The weirdest thing happened, almost like a prophecy. My passenger smiled and told me that her grandmother had once told her that she would be a ninety-two-year-old surfing grandma. And I believed with my whole heart that Anna thought Grandma would surf. Before she got out of the car, we prayed for Grandma's healing and safety while she surfed. Lord, we know that You can make the impossible possible.

"Lord, if it's You," Peter replied, "tell me
to come to You on the water."
"Come," He said…

—Matthew 14:28–29

I'm in downtown Minneapolis in rush hour. Things are moving slow. I'm picking up a man named Deveraux. After a short conversation, I discovered he was from France and had been in the United States for about a year, working in healthcare administration. I told him about my own health struggles and asked if his socialized medicine in France was a good thing or a bad thing.

He replied, "Most people with a serious health issue will come to the United States for quality care, if they have the money."

I smiled and said, "My main source of healthcare is my faith." He laughed and asked if I was serious. I spent the next twenty minutes giving him my story of how faithful God is and that even when it's dark, I have hope in Him. When I got to the airport, he allowed me to bless him and his family with a prayer. He smiled and seemed a little lighter. Thank You, God, for giving me the opportunity to pray for Deveraux and his family. To You be the glory.

He got up, rebuked the wind,
and said to the waves, "Quiet, be still."
Then the wind died down and it was completely calm.

—Matthew 4:29

Not Just Another Day

It's November 8, 2018. I woke up early, knowing exactly what day it was. Twenty-one years ago, I took my wife's hand in marriage. I honestly didn't know, at that time, how much that promise or covenant would mean to me. I may have gone into our marriage not knowing exactly what I wanted and there were plenty of tough circumstances in our first year together, but it didn't take me that long to realize what I needed to do to be a God-honoring man, who put his wife and their lives first.

I stopped at a Caribou Coffee drive-through and ordered up what I needed for caffeine consumption, icy goodness to the last drop. I realized the ringer on my phone was not working. I had to return a couple calls I had missed. The first one seemed familiar, but I couldn't remember who it was until they answered, "Edward Jones, this is Nancy." I had been waiting for this call and from another investment company, to get things moving in my divorce settlement. This is not what I want to deal with today, but I couldn't procrastinate any longer.

I said hello to Nancy and asked for Bob. He was soon on the phone, telling me that I needed to stop by his office and sign some paperwork. I told him I would come right away. The hard thing about going to his office was that

Dawn's business is right next door, literally next to each other in a strip mall, their doors almost touched. I didn't want to see her today, I couldn't get her out my mind or out of my heart. If she was there, I would see her. Anxiety was banging a heavy rhythm on my chest, I had to calm down one breath at a time, I can't do it alone. I need my Uber God.

The Story of Paige

It's a hot Saturday night. I was at church tonight and really enjoyed it. I had spent the last four months going up to the left side of the stage area where the drum set was set up. I had a nice area to sit when I got tired, but tonight my whole revival world was turned upside down or at least flip-flopped from left to right, or maybe right to left, that would depend on which way you're facing. The drum set was gone. I would have no place to sit during worship. A little frustrating, but I could worship from my seat in the third row just as well tonight. Worship and church were good tonight, but I was kind of in a blah-blah mood. I knew I had to work tonight, but it was time to spend time with my Uber God.

My night started right away. I got a short run from North St. Paul over to the East Side of St. Paul. It was a guy and a lady whom I picked up at a biker bar. In just a few minutes I was dropping them off. As soon as I dropped them off, I got another run only two minutes away.

I rounded the corner and pulled up to the address where I was supposed to pick up James. The house was dark, but I could see a light on, at the backside of the house as I pulled up. A few seconds later, I see two people rounding the corner of the darkened house. They both staggered toward my car. The woman was obviously more intoxicated than the guy.

The gentleman stood in front of my window as I rolled it down. He told me that I was driving his girlfriend home. I smiled and said, "That sounds great." I have had issues with really drunk people putting really drunk people into my car in the past. I had to make sure she wasn't going to fall asleep and freak out when she woke up, it happened once before. He assured me that she was fine. The girl must've overheard our conversation and in a very loud voice that I'm sure ticked off the neighbors yelled, "I am fine, let's get my butt home!" She wrapped her arms around her boyfriend, kissed him multiple times, and plopped down into my car.

I asked her a few questions, just to get the ball rolling, but what came next was more than I bargained for.

> Here I am
> On the road again
> There I am
> Up on the stage
> Here I go
> Playin' star again
> There I go
> Turn the page [Paige] (Bob Seger)

Bible Bob

I pulled up in front of Edward Jones and Dawn's business, and to my relief there was no white Nissan Rogue, which Dawn drives, in their parking lot. My breathing slowed. When I had spoken to Bob on the phone, he said he could meet me at my car. He was familiar with my disability and offered this convenience, and I was thankful.

He came out with a clipboard and paperwork; he pointed out where I needed to sign and told me that Dawn had already signed it. I looked at the paperwork and just stared at the dates that were in front of me: November 8, 2018, my anniversary. That in itself was painful, but what stabbed me over and over directly in my heart was her name was no longer the same as mine. She was gone forever. I'll never love anyone like I loved you.

The hurt and shame came flooding over me like lava on an erupting mountain, destroying anything and everything that has life. My hope was gone.

Bob was watching me struggle with my emotions as I attempted to sign the paperwork. He put his hand on my shoulder to comfort me. He leaned forward and asked if he could pray for me. I, with some hesitation, said, "Yes," and he brought forth a beautiful petition for peace in the storms of life and for God's direction. I had never met Bob before, and

I wasn't expecting comfort or love from a perfect stranger, but that's what I got. On this day I was visited by my Uber God when I needed Him most while I sat in the front seat of my parked 2016 Kia Soul, just after driving through the toughest highways of hell.

For a moment, I think I may have felt what so many of my passengers have felt. Thank You, Father God, for letting me experience the other side of Uber God. You are good, even when life is not okay.

Broken World

As we drive through life and we think to ourselves about every person that we meet, "Wow, what a perfect life they have," or "What a messed-up life they have," or "They look very strong," or "They look very happy," or "They look like they have everything put together," or quite frankly, "They look like crap!" Honestly, that is every single one of us at different times. Even when we are not hurting, we are hurting from something from our past.

We have only had one good consistent driving force in our lives, since before we took our first breath (even if we don't know it): the love of our Lord and Savior, Jesus Christ. He never wanted for His kids (us), to ever carry all the crap from our lives on our own shoulders. He died for everything that holds us down: our depression, financial woes, our broken relationships, our illnesses, and, of course, one thing that leads us into a lot of these sad situations: our SIN. He is the answer in all of our bad situations and in all of our heartache.

Come to Me, all you who are weary and
burdened and I will give you rest.

—Matthew 11:28

I know that dealing with the heartache in my own life, the greatest peace that I have received was leaving my sadness and depression, from being kicked in the face and stabbed in the heart, is at the foot of the cross of Jesus. I have to remember to leave the heartache of life with the Creator of the Universe, the only One who can justly deal with it all. I am not alone. Everything I have just said…all have felt, in different ways, at one time or another.

The Walking Man #4

This morning I cleared the rest of my stuff out of my house. I've got a couple things left to grab. I think it's impossible to move and pack all your stuff in just a couple days. I am sure that I will forget things. I've lived here for almost twenty years, it's been my life and my love. Right now, I'm heading back to grab my stationary bike and some pictures and whatever else I find. The sun is shining brightly in my eyes as I head west on the old familiar road to my home.

Through the haze of brightness, I can see the outline of somebody walking toward me. I am not going fast, but my foot softly taps the brakes, and I move up into the shade of a tree. Now I can see him, walking stick and all, standing there, my unknown friend, the walker. Although he has never heard my voice, and I have never heard his voice either, through the years he has been a constant, someone I see all the time and yet I have never taken the time to find out his name. Though my life has changed drastically, some things never do. He was here in the beginning and now he is here in the end. It's a little odd, but I think I know him.

Paige Turned

Through drunken, loud conversation, I could feel she was searching for something she once had. She told me her name was Paige. She was twenty-five years old and had just found out that day that she was pregnant. That took me totally off guard.

She instantly told me not to worry, that she could drink as much as she wanted because she wasn't keeping the baby. My heart fell to my stomach and twisted in knots. I had to speak truth into this situation. I thank God that her being in my car, going 60 miles an hour down the freeway, kind of made her a captive audience. She wasn't going anywhere.

I felt like I had to say something, but I didn't know how to get there. Isn't it cool when God makes a way, when there seems to be no way? Paige would not stop talking. She told me how she had a four-year-old daughter, but her daughter was living with Paige's mom because Paige had just gotten out of treatment. Then she told me that she had been messed up on crystal meth, cocaine, and heroin, but that was all behind her now, she just drinks once in a while. I had to find a way in. I so badly wanted a better life for Paige and her unborn baby. And then the right question and the right answer just happened.

I asked Paige, "Where did you go to treatment?"

She looked up from the backseat and said, "Teen Challenge."

Thank You, Lord, for opening a door. I knew no one could go through Teen Challenge and not know about Jesus. I told her that my pastor once worked for Teen Challenge and I had supported what they had been doing for years. Also, that I had seen the concert choir many times. She, out of the blue, told me that Teen Challenge had saved her life.

I had just stopped at the stoplight at Brooklyn Boulevard and 694. I looked over my shoulder, looked her in the eyes, and said, "God has a plan for you. He loves you and He has never left you. He always wants the very best for His kids, and you are one of His favorites." She instantly broke into tears, sobbing almost uncontrollably. She had been touched by God in the back seat of a Kia Soul.

Almost like a light switch, she turned from a drunk party girl to a broken, sweet, lost, little child, screaming out for acceptance and forgiveness. As I pulled up into a driveway, I asked if I could pray for her. Through red eyes and a snotty nose, she said, "Yes." I prayed that the Lord would give her wisdom and direction. I also prayed that she would feel His love immediately. I grabbed her hand and gave it a squeeze, just before she slid out the door. Earlier in our conversation, she said that Teen Challenge had saved her life. I think Teen Challenge was the vessel used by God to save her life, and tonight, maybe, I was the vessel to save the life of her unborn child. We truly serve an Uber God!

The next morning, I checked my app for comments. This was her statement: "Karl helped me in more ways than one tonight. Thank you so much."

For You formed my inward parts; You knit me together in my mother's womb. I praise You, for I am fearfully and wonderfully made.

—Psalms 139:13–14

Putting It to Bed

My whole body: my head, my heart, my hands, and my feet are all exhausted. The exhaustion that comes with heartbreak is the most devastating and overwhelming type of weariness anyone will ever experience. I was running on empty and I needed some serious filling up.

I thought perhaps spending time with my children would ease my pain, and at the very least cause a distraction to the darkness of my day, but things don't often go the way I had planned. The night before, it seemed my plans to have dinner with my three youngest were all set, but that would change in a blink of an eye: boyfriends, volleyball, work, oh my...and the weather was crappy to boot. This day couldn't get a whole lot worse. I was falling into my own little world of despair. I needed to find a way out, I needed my Uber God. I didn't want to leave my peace, ease, and loneliness (poor me) in my Uber world, but I had to leave the comforts of my car and enter the uncomfortable world of my brothers and sisters, in our fallen reality of revival. We are all broken, but at least we know it.

Once inside, I couldn't stop thinking about how today had really sucked, and how this day, for so many years, meant everything to me, and in many ways still did.

I had only spoken to one person that night about the hardships of that day, but it seemed that multiple people had mentioned something to Pastor Dave that something wasn't right with me. He came over during the service and put his hand on my shoulder and said "We are here for you. We don't know what's going on and we don't have to know. We are all here because we love you, you are a part of our family." And then he went on to talk about the friends who lowered their friend in front of Jesus when there seemed to be no way in. He then started talking about Moses, when Aaron and Hur were there for him, lifting his arms to help the Israelites win the battle that the Lord was fighting for them. It was more confirmation that the Holy Spirit was intervening on my behalf. This was the exact story I was working on for Sunday school that day.

The Lord was doing more than speaking to me, He was screaming in my face, "Karl, I love you, I am proud of you, and I have great plans for you!" He was right there, right next to me, fighting my battles the way He always had. Thank You, my Uber God.

With all the things that are going on in my life, it can be overwhelming, and there are nights when the enemy won't even let me sleep because of worry and fear. The anxiety for me is off the charts. This is when I need to read Jeremiah 29:11 and believe it, and I will, or at least try to believe it. Thank You, my Uber God, for always loving me!

For I know the plans I have for you, declares
the Lord, plans to prosper you and not to harm
you, plans to give you hope and a future.

—Jeremiah 29:11

Worthy of It All

This statement has thrown me for a loop too many times, really from both sides. I've asked myself, "Is everything that Jesus Christ did for me on the cross to redeem who I am, in vain, or is it all part of His master plan?" I know what He did for me wasn't plan B; I was plan A. His word never changes; from the very beginning, He has had a masterful plan for every one of us. Sometimes, we choose not to follow His plan for our lives. I know that I have messed up His plans at different times for my life and sometimes for the people around me. I know God doesn't make mistakes, we do, and that's why, as we go through trials and tribulations in our own lives, the need for that super amazing, all-loving, all-knowing God, who loves us regardless of how much we screw up, just continues to grow.

God loves all of us kids, we as His children need to be ready to step in, to stand in the gap, to be able to hold someone's heart, when they can't hold it themselves. We need to proclaim His truth in our own worlds, and occasionally, or daily, have the guts and kahunas to bring His love that lives inside of us to the broken and misguided people in life. That is the hard part, but it is possible when you love and serve an Uber God.

I was fortunate enough to hear a lot of your stories, and hopefully I could help lead you toward the one true answer to all of our questions. To be honest, at times I'm more confused now about the puzzlements of life, because there are so many more pieces than ever before. But what I do know now is, God has a better plan for me and my life. No one knows me like Him, and no one loves me like Him. He is my Super Uber God!

These are some of the stories of my life and how my Lord and Savior has pulled me through. It would be possible to stretch them out, to put more words on a page, but that's not me. Everything has been poured out to you, from me and from my heart. In the end, I know that everything Christ did for every one of us, was all about Love.

Thanks for reading.

Myself as the Maid of Honor 6 months before
Kathy was upgraded to Heaven

Kathy and I at Age 6

Kathy and I Early Twenties

Life was easier when things were moving slower (Kathy)

The Walking Man, Still Walking

Something to think About

Tips are not required or requested.

- Job

About the Author

Karl has always been very intentional on sharing God with everyone he meets. He believes in the supernatural healing power of Jesus Christ. He has been the go-to guy with his homeless ministry that he had the privilege of starting with the youth from his church, and still does it thirteen years later. He taught Sunday school for fifteen years at North Heights in Roseville, Minnesota, and for the last eight years has taught Native American children at Little Earth of United Tribes in South Minneapolis. He is the proud father of five amazing kids and enjoys life and sharing the love of Christ with passion and humor to everyone he meets.

CPSIA information can be obtained
at www.ICGtesting.com
Printed in the USA
LVHW051606080920
665325LV00006B/492